$\mathcal{J}$UDAISM, LAW & THE FREE MARKET

A N   A N A L Y S I S

JUDAISM, LAW & THE FREE MARKET
AN ANALYSIS

JOSEPH ISAAC LIFSHITZ

— 21 dicembre 2022 d.C. — *grazie!*

ACTONINSTITUTE

JERUSALEM INSTITUTE FOR MARKET STUDIES

Judaism, Law, and the Free Market: An Analysis

Acton Institute
161 Ottawa Ave NW, Suite 301
Grand Rapids, MI 49503

Copyright © 2012 by Acton Institute

ISBN 10: 1-880595-41-9
ISBN 13: 978-1-880595-41-1

British Library Cataloguing in Publication Information Available

Library of Congress Cataloging-in-Publication Data

Lifshitz, Joseph Isaac

   Judaism, law, and the free market: an analysis / Joseph Isaac Lifshitz

Photo Credit: Gianni Dagli Orti / The Art Archive at Art Resource, NY
First Great Sanhedrin (supreme court and legislative body of the Jewish people)
of French Jews in Paris, 9 February 1807, engraving

Printed in the United States of America

CONTENTS

FOREWORD

As one of the world's oldest monotheistic religions, Judaism has accumulated a wealth of knowledge about human affairs over several millennia. Whether it is in the Oral Torah, the Talmud, or the commentaries written by the great twelfth-century Jewish Rabbi, philosopher, jurist, and physician Moses ben Maimon (otherwise known as Maimonides), there are few areas of human endeavor that Jewish religious thinkers have not thoroughly explored as part of their effort to understand the truth about the divine and its implications for the things of this terrestrial world.

Although Judaism did not produce explicit economic texts as we are used to thinking about such things today, Jewish religious figures—especially those spelling out the meaning of the Law for issues touching on property, exchange, economic justice, and the duties associated with charity—did examine in some detail how the tenets of Jewish belief, especially as expressed in Jewish legal thought, applied to activities such as commerce. Closer examination of these questions soon reveals that the contemporary tendency to identify the economic implications of Judaism with modern social democratic principles and priorities is, at least historically and theologically speaking, somewhat difficult to reconcile with many sources of Jewish tradition.

This is one of the theses illuminated in this short book, *Judaism, Law, and the Free Market: An Analysis*, authored by Rabbi Joseph Isaac Lifshitz of the Shalem Center in Jerusalem. To his task, Lifshitz brings many years of close study of the Talmud, Jewish philosophy, Jewish law, and Jewish history. By looking at the treatment of themes such as property rights, charity, justice, welfare, and competition, he demonstrates that Jewish tradition contains a very sophisticated understanding of many of the elements that, taken together, constitute a market economy.

While Lifshitz is very careful not to make overblown or exaggerated claims about Judaism and the degree to which it affirms the market economy, he does show how Jewish religious, legal, and moral principles provide a framework for how to live a good life in the conditions of a market economy. He also illustrates how the same tradition—especially in its treatment of the institution of private property, the duty of charity, and the exhortation to generosity—serves to limit the role of the state in economic life, especially when it concerns assisting those in need. Judaism, Lifshitz stresses, underlines that there are concrete obligations in charity owed to those in need. To deny or ignore these is simply wrong. The same sources, according to Lifshitz, underscore the importance that individuals, families, and communities assume the bulk of the work in assisting the needy, though, he notes, not to the point of creating dependency or discouraging the traditional Jewish emphasis on the dignity of human work.

Jewish and non-Jewish readers of this text will, I am confident, be struck by the wisdom of Jewish religious minds as they have wrestled over the centuries with complex matters such as the place of justice in economic life, the nature and limits of property rights, the virtues associated with wealth-creation, the challenge of poverty-alleviation, and the nature of the development of economic theory. They will, however, also notice that neither Lifshitz nor the Jewish tradition think that market orders are a guarantee of unending prosperity. This is not because of any fundamental distrust of free markets within the right cultural and institutional settings. Instead, it reflects an awareness of the follies of human hubris and the consequences of forgetting that humans should "pray for mercy from Him to whom all riches belong."

Samuel Gregg
Director of Research
Acton Institute

ACKNOWLEDGMENTS

It is with great pleasure that I thank those people without whom this book would not exist.

Primarily, I thank the Acton Institute and the Jerusalem Institute of Market Studies for their initiative in commissioning this book and then helping it to come to fruition. Among the staff of the Acton Institute, I am especially grateful to Dr. Samuel Gregg for his very helpful comments, critiques, and edits that helped to structure the themes and content of the book as it took shape.

I also thank the Shalem Center for enabling me to research and write calmly within its walls. In this regard, I must particularly single out Dr. Yoram Hazony, Dr. Dan Polisar, and Dr. Daniel Gordis.

Special thanks must also be extended to dear friends who have played a background role in shaping the thinking that characterizes this text. First is my colleague and old friend Dr. Joshua Weinstein from the Shalem Center and Mr. Bob Borens with whom I spent so many valuable discussions that generated many of my thoughts. Second are Professor Alan Mittleman, Professor Steven Grosby, and Dr. Simcha Goldin who contributed valuable advice and sources for this book.

My final thanks go to the many students I have taught throughout the years and on whom I "tried" many versions of my ideas, especially Yuval Melamed, Baruch Kundschtat, and Amitay Cohen.

1

INTRODUCTION

R. Ishmael further stated: he who would be wise should engage in the study of civil laws for there is no branch in the Torah more comprehensive than they and they are like a welling fountain.

—*BT*, Baba Batra 175b

As a category of civil law, monetary laws are highly regarded in Jewish tradition. Indeed, over the many generations of Halakhah study, the development of civil law has quite possibly received more sustained intellectual attention than any other Halakhah study. This suggests an initial explanation of why—when it comes to economic theory—study has focused almost exclusively on the legal aspects of monetary exchange. While Aristotle, Augustine, Thomas Aquinas, Bernard Mandeville, and Adam Smith were formulating their thoughts on economic theory, Jewish scholars grappled with the legal framework of economic exchange.

Explicit discussions of economic theory are, however, virtually absent from the Rabbinic sources. It was only in the twentieth century that the beginnings of a distinctly Jewish economic way of thinking began to emerge. This was mostly developed with regard to questions of social justice. Just recently, in the past two decades, some more advanced work in Jewish economic theory has begun to appear, most notably the pioneering work of Meir Tamari, *With All Your Possessions*.[1] Another significant example is Larry Kahaner's *Values, Prosperity, and the Talmud: Business Lessons from the Ancient Rabbis*.[2]

While this contemporary foray into the *terra incognita* of Jewish economic theory may appear to grant a great deal of liberty to its explorers, this is not actually the case for several reasons. Even though no comprehensive work on the subject had previously appeared, the land of Jewish economics was not truly *incognita*. On many occasions, legal disputes about rules tacitly reflect principles or conflicts of principles. While no explicit theory of economics surfaced over the long history of Halakhah development, some basic posture toward economic questions doubtlessly existed below the surface. A serious study of Jewish economic thought must therefore aim to uncover and conceptualize the tacit principles that underlie the system of monetary laws formulated in the Halakhah tradition.

A careful effort of reconstruction is necessary to avoid the error of anachronism. This is perhaps the most difficult obstacle to deducing a theory of economics from Jewish sources. This is further complicated by the fact that economic thought underwent a massive transformation during the Enlightenment, abandoning its descriptive posture for a prescriptive one. Thus, where Aristotle, Augustine, and Aquinas had focused on describing the workings of the economy, Bernard Mandeville and Adam Smith directed attention to prescribing how the economy ought to run.

This change in approach could arise only once the market had come to be perceived as an independent entity. Prior to the modern state's historical emergence, the market was not conceived as an autonomous system susceptible to manipulation. Only when the modern state assumed its present form in the seventeenth and eighteenth centuries did particular Enlightenment ideas about the nature of liberty and equality combine with other concepts to give rise to our present notions of the market economy. It was the idea of the state as a *political project*—as a creation of people rather than simply something that is given—that enabled man to contemplate parallel ways of developing the market. The market came to be understood as a human project that could and should be directed and shaped by man. The idea that an entity as spontaneous as a market could be developed, improved, or regulated by man did not previously exist. Hence, it is not surprising that neither the Talmudic Sages nor the Rabbinic authorities proposed these ideas before they rose to prominence in early modernity. To argue otherwise would be anachronistic.

To uncover the attitude of the Sages and Rabbis to economic theory, it is necessary to search out the legal principles upon which they based their decisions in monetary law. In the first chapter, I examine the laws relating to private property. Jewish tradition is insistent that man can, and should, have a powerful impact on the material world. This idea is based on the biblical notion that man was created "in God's image." Man's role is to have dominion over the world—a dominion that expresses itself through his obligation to benefit from it, to take responsibility for it, and to perfect it through creative acts. As I argue, the ultimate expression of this creative dominion in Jewish thought and law is private property. Private property is thus accorded the sanctity that is so crucial to free-market theory.

In the second chapter, I discuss cases of competition in Jewish law and the broader Jewish tradition. In contrast with its strong defense of private property, I show that the tradition is not as devoted to the free market when it comes to market regulation. In this regard, it cannot be considered "economically liberal." Jewish law permits market regulation, and history shows that regulations were indeed practiced, beginning in antiquity and through to the late Middle Ages. At the same time, deeper study shows that competition was indeed considered a vehicle to prosperity. The sages held that a community has a right to regulate the market, irrespective of whether such regulation would lead to prosperity or not. Nevertheless, it is impossible to avoid entirely the conclusion that the Jewish Sages of antiquity were not fully aware of the vices and unintended side effects of much market regulation.

The third chapter is devoted to idea of charity. At this point, I return to the subject of social justice. Although Jewish law has a long tradition of praising charity, mandating the establishment of charitable institutions, and even coercing charity, charity is considered an act of kindness rather than an act of justice. This means that charity does not redefine property rights. The rich man does not *owe* the needy, and the charity he gives is not a redistribution of his wealth according to justice. Charity is thus done beyond the strict requirements of the law. This means that charity cannot be considered an essential part of the operations of the market, because legally it cannot be understood as an act expressing the human creativity that underpins private property.

The fourth chapter is titled "Generosity." As opposed to charity—an act of kindness performed outside of the market—generosity is understood to describe those acts of kindness that occur within the market. The chapter considers the human investment that successful businesspersons often make in those who have not yet proven themselves in the market. This chapter further examines the distinction between usury and investment and between abusing poverty and helping the needy raise themselves in an honorable way. Here we will see that, already by the high Middle Ages, the business device of apprenticeship played an important role in the development of the economy.

The fifth and final chapter deals with what I term the Hayekian moment. The Jewish tradition did not indeed pass through the phase of Mandeville and Smith. The notion of spontaneous or unintended order can, however, be found in Talmudic tradition, mainly in its definition of the polity. It is my hope that this Jewish concept of spontaneous order will be appreciated as a basis for a more developed idea of the free market and that it can serve as a religious source of inspiration and guidance for a truly free-market economy.

NOTES

1. Meir Tamari, *With All Your Possessions, Jewish Ethics and Economic Life* (Northvale, NJ: Jason Aronson, 1998).

2. Larry Kahaner, *Values, Prosperity, and the Talmud: Business Lessons from the Ancient Rabbis* (Hoboken, NJ: John Wiley & Sons, 2003).

2

PROPERTY RIGHTS
AND THE IMAGE OF GOD

Judaism, it is said, is concerned with caring for the needy. Therefore, it looks to remedy or eliminate the differences in income that are regarded as the true cause of poverty. Because the wealthy tend to be callous and greedy, so the argument goes and, some add, are consequently undeserving of their wealth, they cannot and should not be entrusted with taking care of the poor as in premodern times. Only a state that acts to improve the condition of the poor through taxation, redistribution, and the pursuit of greater economic equality among its citizens, it is argued, can be genuinely considered "Jewish."

This tendency to identify Judaism with the aims of socialism and social democracy is not new. In the nineteenth century, Jewish thinkers found in this activist and often antireligious movement the raw material for the forging of a new, modern Jewish identity. "Judaism—any trace of haughtiness or aristocracy is foreign to it," wrote Moses Hess in 1862. "The Jewish spirit is a social-democratic spirit down to its very essence."[1] Judaism was depicted by many as a synonym for social justice and equality, and the Jews—no strangers to suffering—as the natural bearers of the torch of social reform. As the Labor Zionist leader Chaim Arlosoroff explained in 1916, "The folk socialism of the Jews, the noble spirit of the history of our people, the rule of the ideas of justice and human liberty in the spiritual development of Judaism, the spiritual quality which the Jews acquired over generations, their cultural consciousness and lofty aspiration for freedom—all these empower them to lead the fight for idealistic socialism."[2] It is no surprise, then, that the struggle for economic equality became a central pillar of the new Jewish state's worldview,

5

finding expression in severe limitations and regulations in the sphere of private ownership, on the one hand, and heavy taxation—the lifeblood of the new social order—on the other.

In what follows, I argue that this popular identification between Judaism and social democracy is a false one. As I hope to show, the two central ideas that sustain the socialist redistribution of wealth—the limitation of individual property rights and the dream of economic equality—are alien to both the laws and the spirit of Judaism as reflected in the Hebrew Bible and the Rabbinic tradition. Policies that derive from these principles, moreover, work to undermine a different economic ideal that the Jewish tradition *has* sought to advance. Thus, while Judaism undoubtedly emphasizes concern for the needy—"for the stranger, for the fatherless, and for the widow"—through the commandment to give charity and numerous other precepts, this is not to be confused with the fundamental limitation of property rights in the interests of the poor. It is rare to find in Jewish tradition a call for the restructuring of society or the imposition of economic equality, even as an ideal. Even though classic Jewish tradition has a very strong idea of property rights, redistributionist-like ideas appear in the periphery, such as in parts of the Roman Catholic tradition. The church fathers had a clear view of man's place in the world. The individual's accumulation of wealth for its own sake was seen as sinful, and people's rights to property were not absolute, being limited by, among other things, the needs of the poor. In the classical Christian view, man should not keep more than he needs to live modestly, to fulfill his vocation, and meet his responsibilities. Property was to be made available to the needy, even in extreme cases such as preventing imminent death, in contravention of the owner's wishes.

Jewish tradition takes a very positive view of both the institution of ownership and the accumulation of wealth. It respects economic success, seeing it as both a blessing and the basis of normative life on earth—so long, that is, as it is obtained honestly and proper respect is shown for the social responsibility that accompanies it. In what follows, I explore the basic tenets of Jewish economics, and will make in this context the following three arguments: (1) As distinct from the classical Christian view, which extols self-denial and opposes the excessive accumulation of private wealth, Judaism presents a ideal according to which man must exert control over the material in order to realize his divine potential as having been created "in God's image"; (2) this view is reflected in the Jewish approach to property, according to which the right of individual ownership and the accumulation of wealth is seen as a means of fulfilling man's responsibility in the world; and (3) the obligation to care for the poor stems from this same sense of responsibility and is expressed through the act of *tzedaka*, or charity, in which the individual voluntarily gives away the fruits of his labor out of concern for his fellow man. The Jewish concept of charitable giving does not impinge on property rights but rather expresses the individual's moral duty as a responsible person—a strong and productive individual who provides for himself and his family through honest means, on the one hand, and gives of his time and money out of generosity and a sense of concern, on the other. Charity, in the Jewish view, thus suggests an ideal that differs somewhat from that of classical Christianity—one that flows from a radically different view of man's place in the world and what it means to have been created in God's image.

In order to appreciate the gulf that separates the Jewish economic understanding from the common misperceptions of it, we must first look at the ideas that guided the Catholic traditions of property, wealth, and charity for many centuries before the Protestant Reformation and the rise of the modern era.

SIN AND THE LIMITS OF OWNERSHIP IN CHRISTIANITY

The classical Christian view of private ownership and the accumulation of wealth is grounded in a theology that rejects the idea of man's absolute dominion over the things of this world. As a religion that places God at the center of everything, Christianity insists that God's dominion over the world qualifies man's dominion. However, the measures of the subsequent qualifications depend on the relationship between man and God and the fact that man was created in God's image. Unlike Judaism, Christianity has a doctrine of incarnation, which generates the following conclusion that is not too farfetched: If God became man, then man can, in a certain sense, become "God-like." The question of what this means has been discussed rigorously in the history of Christianity and is closely connected to the definition of the idea of God's image. For Augustine, for instance, the meaning of this idea is the ability of man to come closer to God in heaven, and to serve in the world as a channel of divine grace. Unlike Tertullian who holds that while the image of God can never be destroyed the likeness can be lost by sin (*Bapt.* 5, 6.7), Augustine, presented a more personalistic, psychological, and existential account of the *imago Dei*. The image of God in man orients him to God in invocation, knowledge, and love (*Confessions* 3.12; 13.32).[3] According to Augustine, when Adam was commended to have dominion over the beasts, it was an allegorical commandment to have control over the impulses and thoughts.[4] After the fall of Adam and Eve, man lost his dominion over his impulses and thoughts and by extension over all earthly property. Private property after the fall is thus a result of the expulsion from the garden. The fall set a disruptor in interpersonal relationship as well. Private property is a conventional creation of human society that is instituted in order to help to keep the peace.[5] It was in this spirit that Augustine, writing in the fifth century, responded to the Donatist heretics who complained when the emperor confiscated their property:

> Since every earthly possession can be rightly retained only on the ground either of divine right, according to which all things belong to the Righteous [i.e., God], or of human right, which is in the jurisdiction of the kings of the earth, you are mistaken in calling those things yours which you do not possess.[6]

In other words, while the individual is permitted to possess property for his own personal use, ultimate ownership belongs only to God. Augustine's position went through a change in Aquinas' thought. According to Aquinas, being created in the image of God means an act of contemplation in the intellect.[7] As Janet Colman describes it: "through his reason (Aquinas') man is a master of what is within himself and also he has mastery, *dominium*, over other things, not by commanding but by using them.... Thus man's desire for material goods has only instrumental value, as a *bonum utile*, as means conductive to an end which transcends any use to which property may put."[8] In this way, "Man has no *dominium* over the nature of material things for only God has such *dominium*. But man has a natural dominium over the use of material things to his benefit."[9]

Since Christianity's earliest days, then, individual ownership rights were clear but also circumscribed. By making ownership of property conditional upon its proper use, the church fathers raised the possibility that improper use would cause the forfeiture of one's claim to his own property. Property, inasmuch as it exists at all, exists not as dominion but as *license of use*; if property is misused, the ownership is invalidated, and the property can, in theory at least, be confiscated in order to put it to better use. It follows from this that the unlimited accumulation of property for its own sake is considered wrongful: The one who has more than he needs has too much. Individual wealth is an affront to the principle of the equality of humankind, and an affront to God himself, who in his mercy granted man permission to possess property solely on condition that it is used appropriately. As Augustine writes:

> Do we not convict all those who enjoy things they have acquired legitimately and who do not know how to use them, of possessing the property of another? For that certainly is not the property of another which is possessed rightly, but that which is possessed rightly is possessed justly, and that is possessed justly which is possessed well. Therefore, all that which is badly possessed is the property of another, but he possesses badly who uses badly.[10]

Excess property, or property possessed by one who does not need it yet refuses to give it to the poor, is judged by Augustine to be improperly used. Augustine's teacher Ambrose, one of the fourth century's eminent church fathers, went so far as to say, "It is no less a crime to take from him that has, than to refuse to succor the needy"[11]

By drawing a legal equivalence between refusing to give charity and stealing, Ambrose further circumscribed the boundaries of private ownership, not only condemning the accumulation of excessive wealth but also granting legitimacy to the poor who would steal from those rich who refuse to give of their wealth. In effect, the Church made the forcible appropriation of an individual's property on behalf of the poor a legitimate act.

Ambrose's approach typified much of the early Church's view of material wealth, an approach that was crystallized in the teaching of Isidore of Seville in the seventh century.[12] His view gained acceptance among later Christian philosophers. In the thirteenth century, Thomas Aquinas concluded his deliberations on the subject of property by adopting the teachings of his mentors, according to which property must be defined in terms of an item's use and not in terms of the item itself.[13] Private property has therefore a practical justification. Recognition of the purpose of property is its use for men in pursuance of higher ends.[14] It follows that an item's improper use can nullify the privilege of ownership altogether. For this reason, excessive wealth—the determination of which varied based on criteria such as need, responsibilities, and merit—is akin to stealing from the public. Accumulation of property is allowed only on condition that whatever is not needed be made available to the poor. As Etienne Gilson described:

> [w]e must not forget that by natural law the use of all things is at the disposal of everyone. This fundamental fact cannot be removed by the progressive establishment of private ownership. That each should posses as his own what is necessary for his own use is quite sound a safeguard against want and neglect. But it is a very different matter when some accumulate more goods than they can use under the title of private property. To assume ownership of what we do not need is to make fundamentally common good our own. The use of such goods should remain common ... the rich man who does not distribute his superfluous wealth is robbing the needy of the goods whose use is theirs by right.[15]

Some Christian views of private ownership became more radical as a result of internal Church politics in the thirteenth century. Partly as a response to the Church's emergence as an economic and political world power, Francis of Assisi decreed in 1209 that members of his order would take a vow of poverty—a practice that would become standard throughout many Catholic religious orders. Later this vow would be expanded among many such orders to include a ban on even touching money, except when helping the most needy. Whereas a wide debate ensued between Franciscans and the Church over whether even the Church itself must disavow its vast wealth, there was nonetheless a consensus among Catholics against excessive wealth among individuals.

Catholicism based this approach on a view of man's role in the world as an agent of grace via *imitatio dei*. During the Reformation in the sixteenth century, thinkers such as Martin Luther and John Calvin offered readings of the Hebrew Scriptures that, in certain respects, offer a wider view of private ownership. Nevertheless, during the seventeenth century we find in Reformation circles the idea that the fall put limits on man's dominion of earthy things. Man lost his dominion over animals because of the fall, and his dominion on property was tempered as well.[16]

It is safe to assume, therefore, that in traditional Christian thought in general, the true owner of all property remains God himself. In Catholicism, it is grace and justice that temper man's dominion. In Protestant thought, it is the view that man is inherently and irreparably sinful, and therefore his designs on changing the world must be limited.[17]

Yet, despite the linkages that later developed between Christian thought and socialism, there have been many Catholic and Protestant thinkers who ground capitalistic ideas and free-market institutions upon Christianity. Max Weber in his book *The Protestant Ethic and the Spirit of Capitalism* is known for his contention that for Calvin, prosperity and capital growth counts as an affirmation for the relationship between man and God.[18] Weber understood this theology as a unique product of the Reformation. In Weber's view, work and prosperity were seen as an indication that one was among "the elect." Catholicism, Weber argues, did not need make a similar affirmation and therefore did not produce the same rationale for capitalistic thought and practice.

The Catholic theologian Michael Novak, however, disagrees with Weber. He argues that much Catholic thinking about economic issues was formed in the pre-capitalist world of medieval society that prized stability in economics, politics, and religion. Church teachings were thus more concerned with the just distribution of available goods than with the morality of systems that produce new wealth. Novak goes on to claim that creativity, liberty, and responsibility came to be seen as the answer to the very problem of poverty.[19] Thinking practically for the good of the needy leads, he claims, to a greater appreciation of the importance of private property—a thought, Novak argues, that is to be found in the tradition of Thomistic thought.[20]

Novak's Catholic arguments for free markets do not, however, rely on practical considerations alone. He also points out, from a Catholic standpoint that the human person is an individual who is blessed with a capacity for insight and choice, and therefore he is both free and responsible. Such a capacity is given to man by God. Though man in this sense may appear to be passive recipient of grace, humans nonetheless have these capacities and this ought to be reflected in economic life.

THE JEWISH PERCEPTION OF PROPERTY: DIVINE IMAGE, CREATIVITY, AND DOMINION

What I described as far as traditional Christian ideas of property may sound familiar to anyone who is accustomed to the Jewish tradition. In Jewish tradition as well as in Christianity, we find citations that emphasize that all property belongs to God, and they designate man as the steward rather than absolute owner of property.[21] We can even find Talmudic sources that identify true ownership only in common property.[22]

Jewish tradition insists that man can, and should, have a powerful impact on the material world. This insistence plays itself out in a vastly different view of property rights. Like Christianity, Judaism begins with the idea that man was created "in God's image." In Judaism, however, these words are read in a somewhat different light.

The difference lies in the Jewish tradition's concept of the *purpose* of ownership. Unlike Christianity, Jewish tradition regards the primary purpose of ownership of property not as use but rather as dominium. Though Talmudic sources seek to temper the power of man in the presence of God, it is dominion that they are trying to temper and not with regard to people's relationship with his fellow man but in order to augment the power of God.

Thus, in the Jewish view—and also, interestingly, in Catholic teaching[23]—the body and soul of every person are rooted in the material world. The fact of his alone having been created in God's image, however, elevates his material existence. His inherent godliness sets man apart from all other creatures on earth: he is not merely flesh and blood, but rather a "portion from God above,"[24] an earthly being who contains an element of the divine essence. This unique combination of the human and divine does not mean that man should cut himself off from the material world or direct all his actions toward God; on the contrary, man's place is here, in this world, as an integral part of material existence. Man is obligated to express his dominion over creation, to channel his efforts toward worldly action, and to elevate the material world to a higher level.

Man's dominion finds expression, first of all, through his enjoyment of the good of creation. Whereas the Christian view permits man to derive benefit primarily as a means to the end of what Pope Benedict XVI calls "integral human development," the Jewish sources teach that man is entitled, even obligated, to take pleasure in the world. This is not an endorsement of hedonism; rather, the aim is to enable man to actualize the potential hidden in creation and thereby to bring the work of creation to completion. By benefiting from the world, man infuses it with spiritual content, which serves as a link between the Creator and creation. "If one sees beautiful creatures and beautiful trees," the Talmud teaches, "he says: 'Blessed is he who has such in his world.'"[25] This is not simply an expression of gratitude but an act of elevating the mundane. This is why the Rabbis taught that "man will have to account for all that he sees with his eyes and does not partake of."[26] When we deny ourselves the experiences of this world, even the simplest of pleasures, we cut creation of God off from its higher source and condemn it to a crude, brutish existence. Judaism insists that man should not limit himself to his bare necessities but instead delight in the goodness of the world as an expression of his dominion over it.

Beyond benefiting from the world, however, dominion means that man is also obligated to take responsibility for protecting and preserving it. The Rabbis put it most succinctly in the following parable:

> In the hour that God created man, he stood him before all the trees of the Garden of Eden and said, "See the works of my hands, how beautiful and wondrous they are. All that I created, I created for you. Yet take care not to spoil or destroy my world, for if you do, no one will repair it."[27]

Man is called on to take care of his world because it is given to him as a responsible being. When God created Adam and Eve, he commanded them to "have dominion over the fish of the sea, and over the birds of the air."[28] Indeed, the Jewish tradition makes clear that man's authority over all other creatures is unequivocal. Yet, at the same time, he is enjoined to act responsibly in the material realm. When God placed man in the Garden of Eden, he commanded him "to work it and to keep it"—to derive benefit from it but also to protect it for future generations.[29]

Man's sense of dominion, however, is most vividly expressed not in the benefit he derives from the world or his protection of it but in his unique ability as a *creator*—the most important manifestation of his having been created in God's image. The church fathers held that the world belongs to God, and man in his state of sinfulness has no right to exercise absolute dominion over it. Judaism, however, insists that man is required not only to be involved in the world but also to perfect it through creative acts. According to Judaism, man's creative development of the world is the ultimate expression of his unique status. Man is obligated, to use the idiom of the Rabbis, to "create worlds": So said the Holy One to the righteous, "You are like me ... I create worlds and revive the dead, and so do you."[30]

The power of mankind, according to the Rabbinic view, is nearly unlimited. Like God, who "renews creation each and every day,"[31] man, too, is invested with the supreme power to create worlds. As such, he reshapes reality in accordance with his human spirit—a spirit that in its godliness brings the material world to fulfillment through its elevation. In this way, man plays an integral part in the process of creation, a process that cannot be brought to completion without human intervention. "All that was created during the six days that God created the world," says the Midrash, "still requires work." Even the smallest, seemingly trivial things require man's contribution for their completion. "Even mustard seed must be sweetened, and wheat must be ground."[32] The ultimate act of creation, however, is undoubtedly that of human procreation. Man and woman bring another creative soul into the world, the ultimate expression of human godliness. In this way they, like God, "create worlds and revive the dead," and become true partners in the act of creation.[33]

Man's role, according to Judaism, is thus distinctly informed by the notion that he, having been created in God's image, is to have dominion over the world—a dominion that expresses itself through his obligation to benefit from it, to take responsibility for it, and to perfect it through creative acts.

Judaism, however, does not restrict itself to establishing the role of men as individuals. One of Judaism's central aims is to create a certain kind of society, one that is best suited to man's unique role. This means that the idea of human dominion will express itself not just through theory and parable but also through law. Perhaps the most important legal institution in this regard, which forms the very foundation of society from the Jewish perspective, is the institution of private property.

THE BIBLICAL ROOTS OF PRIVATE PROPERTY

The creation of man in God's image, and his consequent duty to exercise dominion over the world, are the foundations on which the Jewish concept of property rests. In contrast to the classical Christian view, in which ownership is conditional and relates to the manner of an object's use and the owner's vocation and responsibilities, the right to private property in Judaism is nearly absolute and can be restricted only in the most extreme circumstances. In accordance with man's role in the world, it is only through the protection of the individual's property that human beings will be able to actualize the divine image within them and act as full partners in creation.

Property, understood as full dominion over an object, is thus a central pillar of Jewish law, and its protection is a recurring theme in the Bible and the Rabbinic teachings. The significance with which the Torah invests the right of ownership is evident in the numerous prohibitions pertaining to the property of others: (1) the commandment, "You shall not remove your neighbor's boundary mark"[34] establishes the prohibition against stealing land; (2) "You shall not have in your pocket different weights, large or small. You shall not have in your house different grain weights, large or small.... All who do such things ... are an abomination to the Eternal your God,"[35] prohibits the acquisition of property through fraud; (3) "You shall not see your brother's ox or his sheep go astray, and hide yourself from them: You shall surely bring them back to your brother"[36] prohibits the neglect of other people's property even when it is not in your care and obligates the return of lost items. By declaring as criminal anything that results in the loss of other people's property, the Torah emphasizes the importance accorded to the institution of private property. This is expressed as a general principle in a number of verses in the Torah, such as: "You shall not steal" and "You shall not defraud your neighbor, nor rob him."[37] The length to which the Torah goes to encourage a respect for private possessions, however, is demonstrated most sharply in the Tenth Commandment: "You shall not covet your neighbor's house ... or his ox, or his ass, or anything that belongs to your neighbor."[38] Here the prohibition goes beyond the unlawful acquisition of property to include even the coveting of another's possessions.[39]

Further evidence of the high regard in which Judaism holds private property can be found in the punishments that are meted out in the Bible to those who undermine the social order through their flagrant disregard for it. Such, for example, is the attitude taken by the prophet Elijah against King Ahab for his mistreatment of Naboth the Jezreelite in the book of Kings. Ahab is cited repeatedly in the text for his worship of the pagan gods Baal and the Ashera, but his most important sin, for which he is stripped of his kingdom, is the murder of Naboth for the sake of stealing his vineyard. Here the theft is seen as an atrocity, equal in weight to the murder itself:

> And the word of the Eternal came to Elijah the Tishbi, saying: "Arise, go down to meet Ahab King of Israel, who is in the Shomron, in the vineyard of Naboth, where he has gone to possess it. And you will speak to him, saying, 'Thus says the Eternal: Have you murdered, and also taken possession?' And you shall speak to him, saying, 'Thus says the Eternal: In the place where the dogs licked the blood of Naboth shall the dogs lick your blood, even yours.'"[40]

The Rabbinic tradition, as well, emphasized the gravity of acts that violate another's property, equating them with the destruction of the foundations of society. The flood in the time of Noah, for example, was depicted as punishment for the sins of his generation against the property of others: "Come and see how great is the power of thievery," the Talmud teaches, "for behold, the generation of the flood transgressed all, and yet they were not doomed until they stretched out their hands to steal."[41]

The importance of property rights and the societal obligation to uphold them is similarly emphasized in the corpus of legal writings pertaining to ownership. According to the halacha, for example, transference of ownership is valid only when accompanied by an "act of acquisition" (*ma'aseh kinyan*), such as erecting a fence around a property or breaking down a surrounding fence, acts that signify the assumption of new ownership over the property, or at least the previous owner's relinquishment of his claim.[42] An owner's dominion over his property is signified not only by his right to transfer, or to refuse to transfer, his assets to another, but also by his ability to do with his property what he wishes, even if that means its neglect or destruction. This is developed, for example, in a ruling of the Mishna, where it is written that if someone tells his friend, "Tear my garment," or "Break my pitcher," the friend is liable for damages; but if the owner explicitly exempts his friend from damages, the exemption holds, because he is understood to be carrying out the owner's will.[43] While it is possible to debate the details of this ruling, it is clear that everything turns on the owner's will with regard to the object. Ownership, in other words, is understood to be so complete as to include even the right to destroy one's own property.[44]

The definition of ownership as complete dominion is a fundamental principle of Jewish law, the aim of which is to preserve the individual's dignity and sovereignty and to prevent any encroachment on his dominion over his small portion of the material world. The Rabbis of the Talmud, indeed, pushed the matter to the point of hyperbole: "To rob a fellow man even of the value of a *peruta*," the Talmud asserts, "is like taking away his life from him."[45] Indeed, the right to private property is protected even in the most extreme cases. For example, the Rabbinic legend tells the story of King David's deliberations over whether he should set fire to another man's field in order to drive out the Philistines who were hiding there.[46] The Rabbis answer that in all cases in which a person "saves himself through his friend's wealth"—that is, destroys someone else's property in order to save his own life—must nonetheless pay damages. In other words, even in the case of saving a life, which in Jewish law is understood to override nearly every law, one is not exempt from paying damages that result from the actions taken.[47]

Yet Judaism's affirmation of ownership does not end with the protection of property; in many places it also encourages the accumulation of wealth. Economic success is considered a worthy aim, so long as one achieves it through honest means. This stands in contrast to the classical Christian view where the accumulation of wealth for its own sake is rejected and the wealthy are constantly warned about the temptations associated with possession of wealth. "It is easier for a camel to go through the eye of a needle," Jesus says in the book of Matthew, "than for a rich man to enter into the Kingdom of God."[48] In the Jewish view, however, man's obligation to exercise dominion over the world, as a function of his having been created in God's image, brings him to the exact opposite position—an affirmation not of poverty but of wealth. Wealth that is gained through hard work and honest means is, in Judaism, a positive expression of man's efforts as a godly being. "One who benefits from his own labor is greater," says the Talmud, "than one who fears heaven."[49]

This stunning assertion is not meant to denigrate the fear of heaven but rather to affirm the principle that one who turns his talents into achievements is greater than one who neglects his own capacity to strive and create in the world. In the Jewish view, wealth that is derived from hard and honest work is considered a sign of virtue rather than vice; in the Rabbinic teachings, such wealth is the lot of the righteous. Thus the legend says of Jacob, who risked his life to save his property: "Said Rabbi Elazar ... 'For the righteous, their property is dearer to them than their own body. Why so? Because they do not stretch out their hands to steal.'"[50] Worldly wealth, despite having no obvious spiritual content, is even said to contribute to the indwelling of the Divine Presence: "The Divine Presence rests only on one who is wise, strong, wealthy, and of great stature."[51]

Judaism's affirmation of wealth becomes even more striking when one considers its attitude toward poverty. In Rabbinic teachings, poverty is first of all considered a form of pointless suffering. "There is nothing worse than poverty," we find in Exodus Rabba. "One who must weigh every penny—it is as though he bears all the suffering of the world upon his shoulders, and as though all the curses from Deuteronomy have descended upon him."[52] For this reason, Jewish law calls on man to do everything in his power to avoid becoming dependent on his community for his welfare. "There shall be no needy among you" (Deut. 15:4) is understood as an obligation on man to avoid becoming poor, not as understood by some, as a divine promise to negate poverty.[53] That is why Rabbi Akiva taught his son: "It is better to profane your Sabbath than to become dependent on others."[54] From his perspective, man is never excused from taking responsibility for himself and is never allowed to make himself a burden on others. This is not, of course, to deny that poverty also has a value in Jewish tradition. The Sages said, for instance, that "Poverty is good for the Jews."[55]

In light of this view of wealth, we should not be surprised that the Sages exhort all men to earn their living through work. Under no circumstances are the poor to be absolved of their responsibility through the redistribution of wealth. As opposed to the classical Christian view, the property of the wealthy in Judaism is entirely theirs to do with as they wish. Even in a society of significant income differences between the wealthy and the poor, the poor have no *legal* claim against the wealthy. Judaism's concern for the poor, we will see, does not extend to the juridical realm; judges are admonished in the Torah not only never to skew justice in favor of the wealthy but also never to favor the poor.[56] Even in a case of voluntary giving, Jewish law cautions against excessive generosity and forbids a person from donating more than one-fifth of his assets, so as not to become poor himself.[57] This was expressed powerfully in the ruling of Maimonides in his code, *Mishneh Torah*:

> One should never dedicate or consecrate all of his possessions. He who does so acts contrary to the intention of Scripture.... Such an act is not piety but folly, since he forfeits all his wealth and will become dependent on other people, who may show no pity towards him. Of such, and those like him, the rabbis have said, "The pious fool is one of those who cause the world to perish." Rather, one who wishes to spend his money on good deeds should spend no more than one-fifth, so that he may be, as the prophets commanded, "One who orders his affairs rightly,"[58] whether in matters of Torah or in the affairs of the world.[59]

The prohibition against giving too much to the poor is an expression of the Jewish view that there never was, nor will there ever be, an ideal state of economic equality among all men. The Sages emphasized that each man is created differently from his fellow and that this difference is an expression of every individual's uniqueness—of every man having been created in the image of God. Indeed, according to the Jewish approach to property, economic equality is not just impossible—it is also undesirable: Such a condition negates the uniqueness of the individual and therefore negates the image of God within him. Thus, the Bible says, "For the poor shall never cease out of the land."[60] Economic disparity does not demonstrate the moral corruption of society but the fundamental differences among the individuals whom it comprises.

PROPERTY RIGHTS AND CHARITY

Of course, all this raises the obvious question: What, then, will become of the poor? How, indeed, is society to protect the unfortunate individual who is unable to support himself and his family?

Some will inevitably argue that society cannot protect such individuals—that is so strong a concept of property contradicts the obligation to care for the poor, and any society that adopts it will end up abandoning its weakest members to destitution. Yet such a claim misunderstands the Jewish concept of man's role as being created in the divine image. In the Jewish view, man is granted dominion over the world not merely that he may benefit from it, but also that he may take responsibility for it. The legal understanding of property in Judaism is therefore only one part of a broader concept of the role of man in the world—one that plays itself out as well in his duty to care for those in need, through the commandment of charity, or *tzedaka*. As Maimonides explains:

> The term *tzedaka* is derived from *tzedek*, "righteousness"; it denotes the act of giving everyone his due, and of showing kindness to every being according as it deserves. In Scripture, however, the expression *tzedaka*

not used in the first sense, and does not apply to the payment of what we owe to others. When we therefore give the hired laborer his wages, or pay a debt, we do not perform an act of *tzedaka*. But we do perform an act of *tzedaka* when we fulfill those duties towards our fellow men which our moral conscience imposes upon us; e.g., when we heal the wound of the sufferer.[61]

Fulfilling a legal obligation such as the timely dispensation of wages is not considered charity. Rather, charity is something that flows not from a sense of justice but from the goodness of one's character or the generosity of one's heart. The same "image of God" that enjoins man to delight in this world and to exercise dominion over it also obligates him to take responsibility for his fellow man, in particular for those in need. The fact of his being created in God's image indeed gives him the legal and moral basis for keeping his own interests in clear view and striving to advance them by the sweat of his brow. Furthermore, just as the godliness within him encourages man to work and to be productive for his own sake, it also obligates him to care for those who cannot care for themselves. Moreover, it is the affirmation of wealth, the struggle for it, and the legal protections that are given to wealth once it has been attained that make philanthropy a possibility in the first place. If man did not strive first for his own interests, and if the fruits of his labor were not protected, he would have nothing to offer those in need.

For this reason, the Sages defined charity foremost as a moral principle, not a juridical one. Thus, they admonished those who would take money from others in order to give it to the poor: "Better is he who gives a smaller amount of his own charity than one who steals from others to give a large amount of charity."[62]

Again, it is worth comparing this position with the classical Christian approach, according to which, since all men are equal before God, they are all equally entitled to his benevolence. Therefore, those possessions in excess of our needs and responsibilities must be used for the benefit of others, which can include their distribution among the poor. Charity, according to this view, is the means by which man acts as a vessel for God's grace. Because all are equal before God, they are all entitled to the same measure of grace. Christian charity, then, is substantively superhuman and tends to limit the free choice of the individual to how they might use their superfluous wealth to benefit others. Indeed, not only is the individual enjoined to give of his superfluous wealth *because it is not really his*, he is also obligated to give to those who are not close to him, Thomas Aquinas emphasized this point quite forcefully:

> It would seem that we are not bound to do good to those rather who are more closely united to us. For it is written: "When you make a dinner or a supper, call not your friends, nor your brethren, nor your kinsmen."[63] Now these are the most closely united to us. Therefore we are not bound to do good to those rather who are more closely united to us, but preferably to strangers and to those who are in want. Hence the text goes on: "But, when you make a feast, call the poor, the maimed."[64]

In Judaism, the idea of charity focuses on the donor and his relationship with the poor, not on the recipient. Its aim is to cultivate a sense of responsibility, as a moral and religious obligation. For this reason, the rabbis maintained that the donor should favor his relatives over strangers: "When choosing between your own poor and the poor of the city, your own poor come first."[65] By giving to those for whom he feels a special obligation, the donor expresses his self-understanding as a unique individual who takes responsibility for those around him. This kind of giving also underscores the fact that we are talking not about an act of "justice," of satisfying the just claims of the poor against the wealthy but about an act of personal obligation stemming from his sense of responsibility for those around him.

This is borne out by the fact that Jewish legal codes have always placed the laws of charity among religious duties (*isur veheter*), rather than civil law (*dinei mamonot*).[66] Although both categories are equally binding on the Jew, they are two separate worlds within Jewish law. Each has its own set of rules and implications, and each is built on very different legal foundations—such that in the proper study of law, one is not allowed even to draw conclusions in one realm on the basis of examples from the other.[67]

The first category concerns the obligations man has toward God and covers such subjects as *kashrut*, idolatry, and family purity; the second covers man's obligations to his fellow man, such as in contracts and damages. Whereas laws that pertain to the latter category are what make up the system of civic life, their obligations relate to a person's property: When someone signs a contract, he is committing his estate within the context of a social order, and, as such, the courts are permitted to confiscate property in order to effect payment of debts or damages, or to place a lien on his property when he cannot pay. Ritual duties, on the other hand, cover the relationship between man and God, and they fall solely on his moral conscience, not on his property.[68]

Despite the fact that charity relates to one's property, it does not fall into the category of civil law that governs property but rather of religious laws governing moral and ritual obligations. Man is commanded by God to be sensitive to the distress of those in need: "If there be among you a poor man, one of your brethren within any of your gates in your land which the Eternal your God gives you, you shall not harden your heart, nor shut your hand from your poor brother: But you shall open your hand wide to him."[69] Thus R. Joseph Karo, author of *Shulhan Aruch*, included charity in the *Yoreh De'a* section of his work, which refers to religious obligations such as the observance of the laws of *kashrut*, vows, and mourning.[70]

None of this is meant to undermine in any way the importance of charity as a moral duty. On the contrary, Jewish tradition views the commandment to give charity as one of the most important of religious obligations. This sentiment is expressed in the words of Maimonides who wrote in his *Mishneh Torah* that "we must be more diligent in obeying the commandment to give charity than any other positive commandment."[71] As Maimonides further attests, tradition has always found charity to be a staple of Jewish society: "We have never seen nor heard of a Jewish community that did not have a charity box."[72] The point here is that by enshrining it on the moral, rather than civil-legal, plane Judaism expresses a different understanding of the individual's "image of God" than that expressed in Catholicism: Man is encouraged to be a strong, creative, and responsible person; one who builds his wealth so that he may take responsibility both for himself and for those around him.

The essentially religious, rather than civil, nature of charitable enforcement begins with the agricultural laws from which it is derived. It is a moral-religious, rather than a civic-legal, idea that undergirds the laws of *ma'aser ani* (tithing one's harvest for the poor), *leket* (leaving for the poor those sheaves that have fallen behind during the harvest), and *pe'a* (leaving a corner of the field, vineyard, or orchard unharvested for the poor). In none of these cases is there implied a limit to the accumulation of wealth, but rather a minimum of charitable giving as a portion of one's wealth. The religious focus of these laws is underscored, moreover, by their presentation in the Bible and Rabbinic literature together with the laws of *teruma* and *ma'aser*, tithes that support the priests and Levites who are charged with conducting the worship of God in the Temple—in other words, tithes that are ritual in essence. Again, these laws have all been traditionally classified in the area of ritual law (*dinei isur veheter*) rather than civic law (*dinei mamonot*)—meaning that they do not curtail property rights or invoke a notion of civic justice, but they do establish a moral and religious duty to maintain a divine link to the land, to care for the needy, or to support a priestly class.

With the emergence of urban society in mishnaic times, poverty became more widespread among the Jews, and the Rabbis looked to the old rules as a model with which to expand significantly the charitable responsibilities placed on the community. The most important example was the custom of giving a tenth of one's earnings to the poor that was derived from the commandment to give a tenth of one's agricultural yield to the poor in the third and sixth years of every seven-year agricultural cycle.[73] In this way, the Sages set a minimum for charitable giving but also permitted those who could to give more—up to a fifth of their income—a philanthropic system that continues until our own day.

Moreover, the Rabbis authorized the community to compel its members to fulfill their obligations to the poor. The office of the "charity collector" (*gabai tzedaka*) was established and empowered by the community to collect, distribute, and manage its charitable funds.[74] The Talmud, which raises the issue on several occasions, refers to these individuals as "people in authority," or people who are authorized to extract collateral from those who refuse to give to the poor.[75] Indeed, their job is viewed as so important that they are authorized to take this collateral at any time, "even on the eve of the Sabbath."[76]

It is this provision for enforcement that was taken by a number of modern writers as the basis for identifying in Judaism the origins of distributive justice.[77] However, this is an incorrect reading. As we have seen earlier, the central logic of socialism begins with the Christian belief that because it is wrong to have a complete dominium, individual property rights are limited; government, according to socialism, is therefore charged with the duty of redistributing excess wealth in order to limit the economic gaps between rich and poor, leading toward an ideal of economic equality. In the Rabbinic sources, however, coercive authority comes from a different source altogether: not as a means of distribution and justice but as a way of enforcing a minimum level of moral and religious rectitude among its citizens. It is a moral corrective, not an economic one.

Unlike most modern concepts that hold that moral obligations are essentially unenforceable by society, Jewish tradition holds that such laws *are* enforceable, and they in fact have been enforced by communities over the generations. Jewish law recognizes the need to impose moral and religious principles on individuals in order to foster righteousness among citizens and sustain them in the community. The Rabbis called this "setting the boundaries," or *migdar milta*.[78] In this spirit, Maimonides ruled:

> He who does not want to give charity, or gives less than is proper, will be forced to do so by the rabbinical court, even to the point of striking him, until he gives his due, and the court will examine and assess his property in his presence, and take what is proper for him to give. And they may take collateral for charity, even on the eve of the Sabbath.[79]

It is important to note that the use of physical coercion in dealing with rebellious behavior (*makat mardut*) is not restricted to the enforcement of charity but appears in many areas—always, however, as an essentially pedagogical tool meant to bring a wayward individual back to the fold of the righteous. The intended target is not a man's property but his character. We see this same idea in the ruling known as "enforcing to prevent the vice of Sodom" (*kofin al midat sedom*), which holds that an unjustifiably spiteful person—someone who refuses to help his fellow man even though he stands to lose nothing by it—may be compelled to do the right thing. Again, enforcement is aimed at the person's virtue in an effort to set him on the proper moral path. A similar example concerns the vindictive husband who refuses to release his wife through a writ of divorce, despite the fact that their marriage has ended for all intents and purposes. According to Maimonides, if he does not voluntarily give the writ, the courts are authorized to "strike him until he says, 'I am willing.'"[80] Although this view is not universally held by the Halakhah authorities, it is nonetheless derived from a clearly ritual source—a statement in the Talmud according to which the individual may be compelled to bring sacrifices at the Temple even though he does not wish to do so; they should "force him until he says, 'I am willing.'"[81]

The enforcement of charitable giving thus exists entirely on the moral and ritual plane. This is not the same kind of enforcement as the award of damages or the forced fulfillment of a contractual obligation. The aim here is to effect not only justice but also virtue—not to limit one's wealth but to increase personal responsibility. When someone refuses to give charitably, it is not the poor person who files a claim against him; it is the community that seeks to rid itself of wrongdoing. There is no question as to how much money a poor person requires or what constitutes poverty. There is only one question: Is the giver acting as a responsible, moral individual?

CONCLUSION

Judaism praises man's financial independence and encourages him to work hard and to create and enjoy the fruits of his labor, so long as they are obtained honestly. However, Judaism also insists that man should develop a sense of responsibility for his world, including for the plight of the needy. It is this combination of honest labor and the giving of charity that mark the true fulfillment of man's divine nature. Uniquely entrusted with sovereignty over this world, man not only will be strong and independent but will also temper his power with a sense of responsibility.

Thus, unlike the socialist outlook, Judaism holds a fundamentally positive view of individual wealth. Property is an expression of man's sovereignty, his capacity to rule over the material world, so that he may benefit from it, care for it, and perfect it through creative acts. It is the most apparent means through which "God's image" is expressed in human life. It is the necessary and inevitable outcome of man's uniqueness among all God's creatures.

In Judaism, sovereign control over one's property is not conditional on giving charity. The opposite is true: The ability to give charity is conditional upon private wealth. This is reflected in Jewish civil law, which, as we have seen, forcefully defends individual property rights. This does not mean, of course, that Judaism's view of a good society is based solely on the institution of private property, or that it disregards the plight of the poor. On the contrary, Jewish law insists that man take responsibility for his fellow man, show compassion, and give charity. This is only possible, however, when man has full control over his property and is free to accumulate wealth through honest means. Man's responsibility for his fellow man does not impinge on his legal right of ownership; it is a powerful moral demand. Charity is a deed that flows from strength of character rather than the weakness of one's claim to property. It is a mark of responsibility, and as such, it can only have meaning when one has the legal freedom to do with one's property as he wishes.

Is it possible to draw conclusions from this with respect to economic policy? It is fair to suggest that any economic system that sets severe limits on the individual's control over his property, restricts the degree of wealth one may attain through honest means, or undermines his capacity to give charity voluntarily is inconsistent with a desire to enable man to act in accordance with the Jewish understanding of the godliness within him. An economic system based on the systematic redistribution of income with the aim of fostering economic equality is likely to violate many of these basic tenets. By supporting a great portion of its population through transfer payments, such a system encourages dependence and undermines the value of hard work and creative innovation. At the same time, the heavy taxation required to sustain such a system seems to violate the basic right to private property and undermines the incentive to work, innovate, and take responsibility. The Jewish approach seeks to encourage individual responsibility and innovation among society's most successful and its poorest members, for it is in these qualities that man acts as one created in God's image.

None of this is to say that the government cannot create a safety net for society's poor through taxes. If citizens are given the economic breathing room to support the needy through philanthropy, it is legitimate to demand that *all* citizens contribute a minimum amount to that end—perhaps even using the biblical model of a 10 percent minimum of charitable contribution. Regardless of the way it is implemented, what makes a welfare system accord with the principles of a Jewish economics is not that the solution to economic distress be laid solely on the shoulders of individuals, but it be found through policies that encourage a sense of responsibility among all citizens, wealthy and poor. True charity stems, first and foremost, from the goodness of one's heart and not from the mechanism of coercion. In the words of Rabbi Elazar: "The reward of charity depends entirely upon the kindness in it."[82]

NOTES

1. Moses Hess, *Rome and Jerusalem and Other Jewish Writings*, trans. Yeshurun Keshet (Jerusalem: Zionist Library, 1983), 170–71. [Hebrew].

2. Chaim Arlosoroff, "Jewish Popular Socialism," in *The Writings of Chaim Arlosoroff*, ed. Yaakov Steinberg (Tel Aviv: Shtibel, 1934), 3:55 [Hebrew]. See also Nachman Syrkin, *The Jewish Question and the Socialist Jewish State*, trans. Efraim Broida (Tel Aviv: Hakibutz Hameuhad, 1986), 80 [Hebrew]: "The existence of the Jews is a protest against violence, a fight for justice, man's striving to maintain his selfhood. The Jews have embodied a substantial portion of human merit, which would be lost with the destruction of the Jews. The destruction of the Jews is therefore akin to the destruction of humanity."

3. See http://www.vatican.va/roman_curia/congregations/cfaith/cti_documents/rc_con_cfaith_doc_20040723_communion-stewardship_en.html.

4. See Origen, *Homilies on Genesis* 1:11 (*FC* 71:60). See also Peter Harrison, "Subduing the Earth: Genesis 1, Early Science, and the Exploitation of Nature," in http://epublications.bond.edu.au/hss_pubs/51, p. 90.

5. Janet Coleman, "Property and Poverty," *The Cambridge History of Medieval Political Thought, c. 350–c. 1450*, ed. J. H. Burns (Cambridge: Cambridge University Press, 1988), 614.

6. Augustine, *Patrologiae Latinae*, ed. J. P. Migne (Paris, 1844–1864), Letter 133, 12, vol. 33; cited in Richard Schlatter's *Private Property* (London: Allen and Unwin, 1951), 37.

7. As described in Etienne Gilson's analysis of Aquinas:

    This participation in the divine life is in man's case the germ of a new life.... Grace, which is the germ of this life, affects man deeply, regenerating and, as it were, re-creating it. The soul thus affected is still a soul endowed with reason and intelligence. It is because it is capable of intellectual knowledge and therefore of friendship with God, that the human soul is able to receive this divine supernatural gift.... When grace divinizes the human soul it not only re-establishes the balance which had once been destroyed, but causes a new life to spring up, a life freely given to nature. This life participates in the divine and so, by reason of its source, will move spontaneously into the order of the eternal. It is called the "spiritual life," a term which implies that absolute transcendence of body and time which is characteristic of divine things.

Etienne Gilson, *The Christian Philosophy of St. Thomas Aquinas*, trans. L. K. Shook (Notre Dame: Notre Dame, 1956), 345–47. Similar notes can be found in "For Aquinas, the *imago Dei* is the basis for participation in the divine life. The image of God is realized principally in an act of contemplation in the intellect" (*S.Th.* I q. 93 a. 4 and a. 7). See http://www.vatican.va/roman_curia/congregations/cfaith/cti_documents/rc_con_cfaith_doc_20040723_communion-stewardship_en.html.

8. Janet Coleman, "Property and Poverty," 622.

9. Ibid. See also Aquinas, *Summa Theologiae*, II-II, q. 66 a. 1.

10. Augustine, *Patrologiae Latinae*, Letter 153, 6, vol. 33; cited in Schlatter, *Private Property*, 38.

11. Thomas Aquinas, *Summa Theologica*, II-II, q. 66, a. 3.

12. Isidore of Seville adopted the differentiation among natural, national, and civil law as applied in Roman law and expressed in the *Codex Justinianus*. It follows from natural law that ownership is common to all. See Augustine, *Patrologiae Latinae*, 5, 4, vol. 82. However, Isidore did not draw a clear distinction between natural and civil law, nor did he determine a value interface among the different legal systems; see Schlatter, *Private Property*, 41. This omission was later to cause considerable confusion in the canonical law, which was not resolved until Aquinas. Evidence of this confusion can be found in the writings of Isidore quoted in the great collection of twelfth-century canonical laws, the Gratianus collection. On the one hand, Gratianus contends that natural law is the permanent and unchanging basis of law, and every human law that contravenes natural law is null and void. See "Decterum Magistri Gratiani," in *Corpus Iuris Canonici*, ed. Emil Friedberg (Leipzig: Officina Bernhardi Tauchnitz, 1879), Distinctions 5; 6, 3; 8, 1; and 9. On the other hand, he asserts, quoting the church fathers, that common ownership is the basis of natural law. Gratianus does not, however, explain how this can be consistent with private ownership.

13. Aquinas, *Summa Theologica*, II-II, q. 66, a. 7.

14. Colman, ibid. 622–23; Gilson, *Christian Philosophy*, 314. As she describes according to the Summa, Aquinas has a few more justifications for private property: Human affairs are more efficiently organized when each has his own responsibility over his own things, and if not for private property, nobody will take care of things. Men live together more peaceably when each has what suits his own taste; quarrels will erupt were they to hold things in common. See *Summa*, ibid, a. 2.

15. Gilson, *Christian Philosophy*, 315.

16. Philip C. Almond, *Adam and Eve in Seventeenth-Century Thought* (Cambridge: Cambridge University Press, 1999), 116–17.

17. Richard Schlatter, *Private Property: the History of an Idea* (New Brunswick: Rutgers, 1951), chap. 5.

18. Max Weber, *The Protestant Ethic and the "Spirit" of Capitalism and Other Writings*, ed. and tran. Peter Baehr (New York: Penguin Books, 2002), 1–202.

19. Michael Novak, *The Catholic Ethic and the Spirit of Capitalism* (New York: Free Press, 1993), 91–103.

20. See also Thomas E. Woods Jr., *The Church and the Market: A Catholic Defense of the Free Market* (Lanham, MD: Lexington Books, 2005).

21. R. Yaakov B. Asher, Tur, Yoreh Dea, 247.

22. *BT*, Baba Kama 50b.

23. For the Catholic position, see Second Vatican Council, Pastoral Constitution on the Church in the Modern World *Gaudium et Spes* (1965), paragraphs 14–15. See http://www.vatican.va/archive/hist_councils/ii_vatican_council/documents/vat-ii_cons_19651207_gaudium-et-spes_en.html.

24. Job 31:2.

25. Brachot 58b.

26. Jerusalem Kidushin 4:12. See also Nedarim 10a: "If one who afflicted himself only with respect to wine is called a sinner, how much more so one who afflicts himself in many respects."

27. Ecclesiastes Rabba 7:13.

28. Genesis 1:28. This commandment was given to man while he was still in the garden of Eden, and was not altered after he sinned. See also Yevamot 65b; Kidushin 35a.

29. Genesis 2:15.

30. Midrash Tehilim on Psalms 116; see also Genesis Rabba 99: "The Holy One creates worlds, and so, too, your father creates worlds." Moreover, according to the Sages, since man was created in the image of God, his first duty is to create a God-like man—a being in which soul and body merge: "Elazar ben Azaria says that whoever is not engaged in fertility and propagation sheds blood and negates the character according to which man was created in the image of God" Tosefta Yevamot 8:7.

31. Traditional weekday morning prayer, *Yotzer Or*.

32. Genesis Rabba 11:6.

33. Cf. Joseph Isaac Lifshitz, "Secret of the Sabbath," *Azure* 10 (Winter 2001): 85–117.

34. Deuteronomy 19:14.

35. Deuteronomy 25:13–16.

36. Deuteronomy 22:1.

37. Leviticus 19:13.

38. Exodus 20:14.

39. According to the Rabbinic tradition, "You shall not covet" does not apply to thought alone, but rather to the act of bringing unreasonable pressure to bear on one's neighbor in an effort to persuade him to hand over his property, even for monetary compensation. See, for example, Maimonides, *Mishneh Torah*, Laws of Robbery and Loss 1:9. However, even according to this interpretation, it is an extremely significant extension of the principle of private property.

40. 1 Kings 21:17–19.

41. *BT*, Sanhedrin 108a.

42. Mishna Bava Batra 3:3. Some have attempted to define property on the basis of the discussion in Gitin 47b over whether "acquiring the fruits is like acquiring the body," namely, if someone who buys the produce of a field is comparable to the owners of the field itself. It was established that ownership of fruit is not the same as ownership of the object: See Maimonides, *Mishneh Torah*, Laws of the First Fruits 4:6. Some have deduced from this that according to Jewish law, ownership is not determined solely by the right to make use of an object; it is possible to draw up a contract by which one party is the owner of the object and the other of what it yields. Although this may be useful as a figurative example of ownership divorced from usage, it is a mistake to draw a parallel between objects and their yield, on the one hand, and possession and use, on the other. The owners of a field are still entitled to use it for purposes other than its produce. Moreover, ownership of the yield pertains not only to its use, but also to the full possession of that yield.

43. Mishna Bava Kama 8:7.

44. On the strength of this law, Rashi offered an interpretation of the rule cited in Bava Kama 26b, which exempts a man from punishment if he uses a stick to break a vessel that someone has thrown from a roof, while it is still in flight. Rabbi Yosef Dov Halevi Soloveichik, author of *Beit Halevi*, explained: "As has previously been said, if someone threw a vessel from the roof and someone comes along and breaks it with a stick, he is not liable. Why so? He broke that which was already broken." Rashi adds on this case: "The owner of the vessel threw the vessel," he and no other. Rashi's insistence on this point is difficult to understand because if the vessel is thrown by its owner from the top of the roof then it must be considered to have been abandoned, and there is no liability for damaging an abandoned object. The most likely answer is that by throwing the vessel, the owner demonstrated his ownership by doing with it as he pleased. Ownership in this case is shown not by the use of the vessel but by its deliberate willful destruction. Rabbi Yosef Dov Halevi Soloveichik, *Responsa of the Beit Halevi* (Vilna: Yosef Rubin, 1863), 1:24; 2:7 [Hebrew].

45. Bava Kama 119a.

46. Bava Kama 60b.

47. The single exception to this rule is the king, who is granted a special dispensation to confiscate or damage private property during an emergency without having to make restitution, insofar as he is acting for the public good. See Maimonides, *Mishneh Torah*, Laws of Damage 8:2; R. Joseph Karo, *Shulhan Aruch, Hoshen Mishpat*, 388. According to Rashi, moreover, one man must sacrifice his life rather than damage someone else's property. See Rashi on Bava Kama 60b, s.v. *vayatzileha*: "He may not burn it [even in order to pay afterwards] since it is forbidden to extricate himself by paying for it to be reinstated." In contrast, see *Responsa of Rabbi Solomon ben Aderet* (Jerusalem: Or Hamizrach Institute, 1998), 4:17 [Hebrew]: "He may certainly save himself in order to pay." See also Yoma 83b: "I deprived the shepherd and you deprived the entire city."

48. Matthew 19:24. See also Vernon Bartlet, "The Biblical and Early Christian Idea of Property," in *Property, Its Duties and Rights: Historically, Philosophically, and Religiously Regarded*, ed. Charles Gore (New York: Macmillan, 1922).

49. *BT*, Brachot 8a.

50. *BT*, Hulin 91a.

51. Shabbat 92a.

52. Exodus Rabba 31:14.

53. *BT*, Baba Mezia, 30a; ibid 33a; Sanhedrin 64b; Rashi Sanhedrin 64b Sanhedrin 64b.

54. *BT*, Pesahim 112b.

55. *BT*, Hagiga, 9b.

56. Leviticus 19:15.

57. Cf. *BT*, Ketubot 50a: "One who donates should not donate more than one-fifth lest it should be needed for others; and there is a story about one who wanted to donate [more than one-fifth] and his friend did not let him." See also Karo, *Shulhan Aruch, Yoreh De'a* 249:1.

58. Psalms 112:5.

59. Maimonides, *Mishneh Torah*, Laws of Oaths and Vows 8:13.

60. Deuteronomy 15:11.

61. Maimonides, *Guide for the Perplexed*, trans. M. Friedlander (New York: Dover, 1956), 3:53, 393. By contrast, see Ephraim Frisch, *An Historical Survey of Jewish Philanthropy* (New York: Macmillan, 1924), 77. Frisch remarks on the etymological connection between charity and righteousness, which he says arose from a change of meaning between the language of the Bible and that of the Sages. The meaning of *tzedaka* in the Bible is righteousness, meaning an attribute of a righteous person, whereas in the Rabbinic literature it refers to the giving of charity to the needy. See also Tamari, *With All Your Possessions*, 36: "The divine origin of wealth is the central principle of Jewish economic philosophy. All wealth belongs to God, who has given it temporarily to man, for his physical well-being"; p. 52: "The 'haves' in Judaism have an obligation to share their property with the 'have-nots,' since it was given to them by God partly for that purpose."

62. Ecclesiastes Rabba 4:6. One of the exceptions is *Sefer Hasidim*, from which it emerges that the wealth the rich man accumulates is considered robbery:

> If the Holy One gives wealth to the rich man and he does not give to the poor, then he gives to one what could have provided for a hundred and the poor come and cry out before the Holy One, "You gave to him what could have provided for a thousand and he provided me no benefit." And God makes a calculation with the rich man as if he had robbed many and says to him, "I gave you wealth so that you could give according to your financial means to the poor and you did not give, so I will take back from you as if you had committed robbery and as if you abused my deposit because I put wealth into your hands so that you could distribute it to the poor and you appropriated the wealth for yourself."

Rabbi Yehuda Hehasid, *Sefer Hasidim* (Berlin: Mekitsei Nirdamim, 1891), 331, n. 1345, [Hebrew]; on the Christian spirit pervading this passage see Yitzhak Baer, "The Socio-Religious Tendency of *Sefer Hahasidim*," *Zion* 3 (1938): 29 [Hebrew].

63. Luke 14:12.

64. Aquinas, *Summa Theologica*, II-II, q. 31, a. 3.

65. Mechilta d'Rabbi Ishmael, Masechta Dechaspa Mishpatim, chap. 19; Bava Metzia 71a.

66. Menahem Elon, *Jewish Law: History, Sources, Principles*, trans. Bernard Auerbach and Melvin J. Sykes (Jerusalem: Jewish Publication Society, 1994), 1:122:

> Although all parts of the halacha are rooted in the same source, share the same principles and methods of analysis, and provide and receive reciprocal support, nevertheless, study of the halachic sources reveals that the halacha did make very fundamental distinctions between its two major categories, namely, monetary matters (that part of the halacha included in the concept of *mamon*) and non-monetary matters (that part of the halacha included in the concept of *isur*).

67. *BT*, Ketubot 40b, 46b; *BT*, Kidushin 3b.

68. *BT*, Bava Metzia 30b. On this subject, Menachem Elon, the foremost authority on the application of Halakhah jurisprudence to Israeli law (*mishpat ivri*) and a former justice of Israel's Supreme Court, wrote as follows:

> The failure to perform a civil norm [in Jewish law] is subject to judicial sanction, and a court will enforce compliance; not so a moral imperative—this is a matter for the individual himself, between God and conscience. The juridical realm does not involve itself in the performance or lack of performance of purely moral obligations and certainly does not enforce compliance. (Elon, *Jewish Law*, vol. 1, 141)

See also on the question of the distinction among law, religion, and morality in the responsa of Rabbi Yehiel Jacob Weinberg, in *Seridei Esh* (Jerusalem: Mosad Harav Kook, 1977), pt. 1, n. 65 [Hebrew]:

> And now I will raise a general matter: It is well known how hard learned jurists strove to discover the dividing line between law and morality, or between law and equity. Books in foreign languages have already been written on the subject. And note that in the laws of Israel we have found explicit in Bava Metzia 83a

in the story of the wine carriers: "He said, 'Is that the law?' He inquired. 'Even so,' he rejoined: 'That you may walk in the way of good men.'"

See also *BT*, Ketubot 49b concerning the duty of a son to sustain his father.

69. Deuteronomy 15:7–8.

70. Rabbi Joseph Karo, *Shulhan Aruch, Yoreh De'a* 248:1. The commandment to act beyond what is required by the law is generally considered to be a sign of piety. See Maimonides, *Mishneh Torah*, Laws of Murder and Preservation of Life 13:4: "But if one is pious and does more than the letter of the law demands, even if he is a prince of the highest rank, still if he sees another's animal crouching under its burden of straw or sticks or the like, he should help unload and reload." See also Maimonides, *Mishneh Torah*, Laws of Robbery and Loss 11:7. On the other hand, the enforcement of selfless behavior is not a measure of piety but the policy of the Rabbinical court and is a specific example of a ruling on moral and not legal grounds, in accordance with the instruction to the Rabbinical court to educate the people and preserve the principles of religion and morality. See Maimonides, *Mishneh Torah*, Laws of the Sanhedrin and the Punishments Meted Out 24:4. The obligation to behave in a selfless manner has the authority of the Talmud (e.g., Bava Kama 21b) and Maimonides: "Thus also in all instances where one benefits while the other incurs no loss thereby, the latter is compelled to accede to the demand of the former." *Mishneh Torah*, Laws of Neighbors 7:8.

71. Maimonides, *Mishneh Torah*, Laws of Gifts to the Poor 10:1.

72. Maimonides, *Mishneh Torah*, Laws of Gifts to the Poor 8:3.

73. See Rabbi Meir of Rothenburg, *Responsa of the Maharam Ben Baruch* (Prague Press), n. 75, s.v., "And to distribute his wealth [to his children]." See also Rabbi Moses Isserlis' commentary on *Shulhan Aruch, Yoreh De'a* 249:1, and the commentary of Rabbi Shabtai ben Meir Hakohen (*Shach*) ad loc. sub-clause 3.

74. Mishna Demai 3:1; Mishna Kidushin 4:5; Mishna Bava Kama 10:1; cf. Jerusalem Pe'a 1:1.

75. See, for example, the discussion of this question in Bava Batra 8b.

76. *BT*, Bava Batra 8b.

77. Ze'ev Falk, *The Values of Law and Judaism: Towards a Philosophy of the Halacha* (Jerusalem: Magnes, 1980), 117, 119 [Hebrew]; Dagan, "Laws of Wealth Creation," 178–90; Shimon Federbush, *Laws of the Kingdom in Israel* (Jerusalem: Mosad Harav Kook, 1952), 23–25, 126–28, 138–40 [Hebrew]; Aharon Lichtenstein, "A Clarification of *Kofin al Midat Sedom*," in *Jewish Philosophy in America*, ed. Menachem Zohari, Aryeh Tartakover, and Haim Ormien (Tel Aviv: Brit Ivrit Olamit, 1973), 380–81 [Hebrew]; Tamari, *With All Your Possessions*, 36–38, 52–56, 210–11, 240, 242–43, 248–49, 277; Frisch, *Historical Survey*, 77, 80; Walzer, *Spheres of Justice*, 3–6, 75–78, 92.

78. *BT*, Yevamot 90b. According to this moral principle, Rabbi Isaac ben Avraham, one of the great twelfth-century Tosafists, compared the duty of charity to that of honoring one's father and mother. See Tosafot to Bava Batra 8b, s.v. *akfeh lerav natan*; see also

Rabbi Nisim Gerondi on Ketubot 18a; Nachmanides on Bava Batra 8b. For more on Rabbi Isaac ben Avraham, see Ephraim E. Urbach, *The Tosafists: Their Lives, Writings and Methodology* (Jerusalem: Bialik Institute, 1996), 261–71 [Hebrew].

79. Maimonides, *Mishneh Torah*, Laws of Giving to the Poor 7:10. Regarding the enforcement of moral laws in the form of *migdar milta*: "The court is empowered to flog him who is not liable for flagellation and to mete out the death penalty to him who is not liable for death. This extensive power is granted to the court not with the intention of disregarding the law, but in order to build a fence around it" (Maimonides, *Mishneh Torah*, Laws of the Sanhedrin 24:4).

80. Maimonides, *Mishneh Torah*, Laws of Divorce 2:20.

81. *BT*, Bava Batra 48a.

82. *BT*, Succah 49b.

3

SOCIAL WELFARE IN TALMUDIC LAW

When studying the philosophy of property ownership in Jewish law (*Halakhah*), the issue of distributive justice invariably comes up. Even those who refrain from associating Judaism with socialist ideals explicitly use Jewish law's approach toward the roots of ownership to determine the principles behind the relationship between society and the individual in Judaism.[1] Other scholars point to Jewish Law's commitment to principles of social justice, which allows the individual his liberties up to a certain point and at the same time obliges him to be socially responsible and to engage in give-and-take with others.

Such claims are based on the limitations placed by Jewish Law on personal ownership, the land-connected commandments of aid to the poor, and the custom of Jewish communities to enforce charity giving. The prohibition against working the land in the Land of Israel during the Sabbatical Year, and the obligation to return land to its original owners during the Jubilee Year, suggest that Judaism does not consider the individual to be absolute master over his possessions.[2] A similar claim has been heard concerning distributive justice, based on the explanation of the rule of *kofin al middat Sodom* (literally: coercing over the trait of Sodom), according to which an owner's unwillingness to help another person is overridden by a court of law if he himself will not lose anything by complying.[3]

This discussion has led to the conclusion that the Jewish concept of ownership rejects the view that people are absolute masters of their possessions because it limits the right to private property when a social cause is involved. Both the claim and the conclusion are expressed in the following quote from Rabbi Aharon Lichtenstein:

> Coercion over the trait of Sodom completely contradicts the widespread
> idea that man is the supreme ruler over his possessions, that his property is
> his to do with it as he pleases; as long as he is not causing direct damage to
> another person, no one can hinder him. Jewish Law has a different spirit to
> it.… In Jewish Law there is almost none of the aversion to private property
> that the Church Fathers expressed.… But Jewish Law never idolized this
> concept, and other moral necessities may occasion its limitation. Though
> Jewish Law is extremely removed from Proudhon's statement that "Property
> is theft," on the other hand, it refuses even to agree with the popular expres-
> sion that "An Englishman's home is his castle." … We must differentiate
> between ownership for the sake of usage and ownership for the sake of
> sovereignty; we must agree with the first statement, and condemn the latter.[4]

On the other hand, the radicals claim that charity, the commandments relating to
the land, and the matter of forcing a person to help his fellow if he himself is not
inconvenienced by it all indicate Jewish Law's so-called social agenda. According
to these radicals, Jewish Law is not satisfied with placing general limitations on the
right to private ownership. Instead it demands its implementation in a redistributive
policy applicable to the possessions in society, the goal being to decrease poverty
or even do away with it altogether. As one commentator writes

> The basic direction of the Torah was to create in the Land of Canaan a model
> human society, in which human equality and equal economic subsistence
> will be ensured to all. This aspiration was expressed in the slogan, "There
> will be no destitute people among you," meaning that the political regime
> must engage in a fair distribution of property, in order to prevent the creation
> of a class of economically-destitute people.[5]

In this context, charity was seen as one of the expressions of a social plan for
balancing class gaps. It seems that all property belongs to God, and man is entrusted
with it for his own use and for sharing it with the needy. A claim repeated time and
again is that the word *tzedaka* (charity) and *tzedek* (justice) are one and the same:

> Indeed, the term *tzedaka*, coined from the word *tzedek*, shows us that char-
> ity is not a matter of merely generosity or pity, but is seen as a matter of
> honesty and justice, and is an obligation placed on man. Not for nothing do
> we find the terms *tzedaka* and *mishpat* (judgment) together in many places
> in the Bible. And already when speaking of the descendants of Abraham
> our Forefather, it says "And they will keep the way of God, to do *tzedaka*
> and *mishpat*."[6]

It must be noted that this claim is not completely accurate, for the word *tzedaka*
in the Bible is merely a different form of the word *tzedek* and is not the same as
the term *tzedaka* in the language of the Talmudic Sages and in modern Hebrew.[7]
According to one of these opinions, the dynamics of the commandment to give char-

ity brings about the transfer of the individual's personal obligation to the society as a whole, and then the society is permitted to collect funds from its members beyond the sum they are obligated to as individuals—and not only as a moral obligation but with the goal of establishing social justice.[8] Likewise another opinion holds that charity is proof of Jewish Law's social policy, which is binding on the social organization and obligates it to engage in distributive policies according to equal basic needs determined by the society's culture and resources.[9]

It should be noted that the idea of distributive justice is essentially Aristotelian in nature. According to Aristotle, the principles of justice pertain as much to society as to the individuals and, in the case of distributive justice, focus on realizing a fair division of social and economic resources. Any individual who wishes to behave justly must contribute his part to society and act in a way that will be beneficial to its overall effective functioning. The moral obligation is not placed on the individual as such and certainly is not dependent on his whims. The idea of distributive justice opposes an individualistic approach toward justice, as well as the idea that moral decisions should be made by each individual separately. In between these two extremes, there are intermediate viewpoints that integrate collectivistic approaches regarding distributive justice with individualistic ones.

The attempts of social commentators to prove the value of Jewish Law as a relevant social message would have been praiseworthy if only they would have not taken such an extreme stance regarding distributive justice. This has led them to misrepresent Jewish Law's approach. Their conclusions are based on a selection of sources that are presented as the social manifest of Jewish Law but that ignore other sources from which other conclusions arise.

This chapter illustrates how Jewish Law does not present the limitations on the right to private property and the individual's obligation to be considerate of others as two sides of the same coin. In other words, Jewish Law does not put charity to the test of rivalry. Indeed, while Jewish Law sometimes limits the individual's mastery over his possessions, it does not do so from a stance of distributive justice and does not place these limitations within its judicial system. The wealthy man's moral conscience does not translate into a judicial right of the needy person, and the needy person—and society in his name—may not demand anything from him. Moreover, we will see that the effort to find distributive justice misrepresents the Talmudic approach to social welfare and the process of development of the concept of welfare as expressed in Jewish communities in the Middle Ages.

THE RELIGIOUS LIMITS ON PROPERTY

Where, then, do the limitations on property rights come from, and how can they be reconciled with the legal definition of ownership as sovereignty over property? Jewish Law's complex attitude to property rights is connected to the complex relationship between man and God. Limiting man's freedom in face of the divine reflects the unequal relationship between them. Curtailing man's mastery over his possessions is derived solely from man's religious obligation and not from his status *vis-à-vis* another human being. His rights over his property are limited by the religious obligation to leave the land fallow on the Sabbatical Year, and to return land to its owner during the Jubilee. Similarly, acting in accordance to the trait of Sodom is considered to be a defiance of a religious value; it is construed as a tendency to identify with the values of the city of Sodom, the moral antithesis of Jewish Law.[10] So, too, giving charity is a religious norm, one that channels the natural God-given tendency to be merciful into personal responsibility and generosity; this in no way lessens a person's mastery over his possessions.

All the limitations placed by Jewish religious law on property rights are of a moral nature—they have no legal or monetary standing, and there is nothing in them that changes the legal definition of property rights. Hence, any interpretation that claims the existence of distributive justice in Jewish Law as separate from the individual's religious identity, and defines individual obligations in legal terms and not in moral ones, must be merely a reduction of Jewish Law's theological principles to an anachronistic political position, and, in doing so, also distorts the judicial principle.

Public responsibility regarding charity giving arises from viewing the Jewish people as a religious body whose existence as a collective group has intrinsic meaning. The Jewish people, collectively, has a covenant with God and is committed—as a people—to Torah values; it is also obligated to force the individuals within the collective to perform those commandments that apply to them as individuals.

The collective itself has its own obligations. The obligations of each individual are translated therefore into collective obligations as well, due to the collective's obligation to force individuals to observe the commandments. This is how Maimonides defined the obligation to perform the commandment of giving charity, seeing one's belonging to a religious collective as the root of this commandment:

> All of Israel and those who join them are like brothers, for it says, "you are children of the L-rd, your God." If a brother will not have mercy on his own brother, who will have mercy on him? And to whom do the poor of Israel look to? To the non-Jews who hate them and persecute them? Obviously, they look only to their brethren.[11]

The background to this outlook is the *midrash* on the continuation of the verse quoted by Maimonides: "'*Lo titgodedu*'—*lo ta'asu agudot agudot*" (You shall not cut yourselves—you shall not make divisions among you).[12] There is a commandment to avoid divisiveness among the people. Maimonides saw unity and mutual obligation toward others as a primary factor in the survival of the Jewish people as a nation.

A similar opinion was expressed by the supreme authority in Jewish Law in Western Europe in the thirteenth century, the Maharam of Rothenburg. Like Maimonides, he saw the nation as a religious entity, with all the communal administrative efforts, including organizing charity giving, aimed toward the goal of preserving and upholding the nation's spiritual and physical existence:

> All residents of the city are considered partners in the city's wall, its cavalry, guards, armory, gate maintenance, soup kitchen and the charity collection. And since the residents are partners, we have a tradition that no partner can break up a partnership without the other partner's agreement. And even if the matter is in contradiction to the law of the Torah, since [the communities] in the kingdom have the custom of defining themselves as partnerships, it is forbidden to divide the community, for if every person would separate himself, [all] would come to do bad things, for every one would divest himself of a responsibility and place it on his fellow, and [it would come] to great and endless quarrels ... for we wish to be one people and a unified group, and ... be able to exist among our enemies.[13]

In demanding that every individual in the community fulfill his obligation of mutual responsibility in order to become "a unified group," the Maharam is indirectly referencing the saying of the Talmudic Sages, *lo ta'asu agudot agudot*. That is why Maimonides and the Maharam saw the commandments of mutual assistance and the concern for the poor as ones that preserve Jewish existence on two levels: The fulfilling of a moral obligation expresses the Jewish spiritual ethos, and the mutual help enables the continued physical existence of the Jewish people. Thus the existence of the political entity is demanded by the religious entity and nourishes it.

THE CONCEPT OF WELFARE IN THE TALMUD

The concept of welfare in the Talmud leans, to a great extent, on the agricultural-social commandments as they appear in the Bible. There are almost no commandments to give charity that are not connected to agricultural produce. That being said, the Torah does specifically command to give charity to the poor and forbids ignoring their distress:

> If there shall be a destitute person among you, any of your brethren in any of your cities, in your land that the Lord, your God, gives you, you shall not harden your heart or close your hand against your destitute brother. Rather, you shall open your hand to him; you shall lend him his requirement, whatever is lacking to him. (Deut. 15:7–8)

Besides this commandment and others that demand that one be considerate of the poor when it comes to legal actions and collecting loans, the Torah does not mention the commandment to donate money to the poor many times.

On the other hand, the Torah does mention many agricultural-social commandments. It commands to leave a *pe'ah*—a corner—of the field for the poor, to leave them also *leket* (stray wheat stalks that fall from the hand of the harvester) and *shichechah* (stray bushels left behind in the field). A further commandment is to leave to the poor the small bunches of grapes as well. The Torah also commands to set aside one tenth of the crops for the poor in the third and sixth years of the Sabbatical Year cycle.

It is possible that until the time of the Mishnah, these measures were sufficient for a basically agricultural Jewish society when it came to supporting the destitute. However, the changes wrought by the Hellenistic period, specifically the creation of an urban society, caused the poor to lose their sources of livelihood. The Sages subsequently expanded the commandment to give charity; it became not only a matter of providing food for the needy but also giving money and other means of subsistence.

The changing of the commandment to give charity from one that has a connection to agricultural life, to one connected to urban living, is what seems to have added a public aspect to such actions. This was the background to the appearance of the institution of charity collectors (*gabba'ei tzedaka*) and the right of the community to force individuals to give charity in the Mishnah and the Talmud. The term *gabbai tzedakah*—charity collector—appears already in the Mishnah[14] and the Tosefta,[15] as a known entity, and there are rules laid down regarding ethics and transparency. Talmudic law even mandates the establishment of a charity organization in every town:

> Any town that does not have the following ten things, no Torah scholar is
> permitted to live in it: the court flogs and punishes, and charity is collected
> by two and distributed by three, and a synagogue, and a public bath, and
> a lavatory, a doctor, and craftsman, and scribe (and cook), and a teacher
> for the young children.[16]

This law recommends above-board distribution of charity and determines the number of people required for it. At the same time, we should also note the authority given to these collectors and the placing of their role within the context of the public's obligation to care for the needy. The collectors are given a certain degree of authority to enforce their collecting, and the Talmud even calls them *ba'alei serarah*—bearers of authority, for they have the authority to take collateral from those who refuse to give to the poor "even on the Sabbath eve (= Friday)."[17] The role of the collector was to encourage the individuals to give charity and then to collect it and to distribute it. This task was dealt with by a number of authority-bearing people, as stipulated by Jewish Law when describing the establishment of a special court of justice that was placed in charge of the collection and distribution of charity:

> The [charity] fund is collected only by two, for one may not invest [people]
> with the power to collect funds unless there are two … and it is distributed
> only by three, because it is like monetary cases, for they give each one his
> needs for the Sabbath. Food for the soup kitchen is collected by three, for
> it is not a set thing, and is distributed by three.[18]

Many Jewish laws in the Talmud guide the appointment and behavior of charity collectors. They must have a good name and lineage. They are also commanded to conduct themselves particularly honestly, in a way that raises no suspicion of their having embezzled any of the money intended for charity.[19] Two charitable institutions were established in the cities: the charity fund and the soup kitchen. Money was donated to the fund, and food to the soup kitchen. In this way, basic subsistence was guaranteed to every needy person.

The commandment to give charity is described as an obligation that is binding on any person, regardless of his social status and economic situation. Even a poor person who himself is supported by the charity fund is obligated to give to others. The pain and distress of the needy should touch everyone's heart and cause them to give of their money to him. The establishment's work for the poor people's welfare does not exempt the individual from his moral obligation to care for the needy.

THE CUSTOM OF A MONETARY TITHE

In the Middle Ages, welfare institutions were an inseparable part of the Jewish community. As Maimonides testifies: "We have never seen nor heard of a community of Jews that does not have a charity fund."[20] One of the notable examples is the acceptance of the custom to give one-tenth of all profits to the poor, modeled upon the mitzvah of *ma'aser ani* (the obligation to give the poor one-tenth of the agricultural produce in the third and sixth years of every Sabbatical cycle). This obligation set a minimal standard for charity, and allowed anyone who wished to do more to give up to one-fifth of his profits. This institutionalized view did not, however, uproot the role of private charity. The community collected a welfare tax from its members and, at the same time, recognized the right of every individual to give charity to his family members and to other needy people according to his own wishes. Therefore, the community did not collect the full sum that it was entitled to from every individual, so that he would be able to fulfill his obligation by giving to his relatives as well.

The connection between the custom of a tithe taken from money and the land-based commandments arises from the custom of devoting one-tenth of the profits to charity, which was apparently common in the Middle Ages. One of the examples is a Tosafot that quotes a *midrash* who extrapolates from the verse that contains the commandment to tithe the crops the obligation to set aside one-tenth even from nonagricultural profits:

> It says in the *midrash* in the Sifrei: "'You shall surely tithe the entire crop
> of your planting, the produce of the field, year by year.'—I have only the
> crop of your planting that is obligated in a tithe. How do we know that
> interest and trade and all other types of profits [are also included in this
> obligation]? It says 'the entire [crop]'; it would have been enough to say 'the
> crop.' Why does it say 'the entire'? To include interest and trade anything
> else that profits a person."[21]

The Tosafot attribute this *midrash* to the Sifrei. In the Sifrei that is extant today, this *midrash* does not appear, but in the Peskita D'Rav Kahana similar things are said:

> "You shall surely tithe" (Deuteronomy 14:22), so that you will not be caused loss. Tithe so that you will get rich. The Holy One, Blessed be He, said: Tithe what is mine, and I will tithe what is yours. "The entire"—R. Abba bar Kahana said: this hints to the traders and the seafarers that they should separate a tenth for those who labor in Torah.[22]

The custom of a monetary tithe was apparently common in Western Europe even before the thirteenth century, since the Sefer Chasidim mentions it,[23] as well as R. Isaac of Vienna who brings as a source for this the *midrash* that promises blessing to he who is careful to tithe his produce:

> In the first chapter of [tractate] Ta'anit [it says]: R. Yochanan says: "What is the meaning of the commandment from Deuteronomy (14:22) *aser te'aser* (You shall set aside every year a tenth part of all the yield of your sowing)? Tithe so that you should be rich (a play on words—te'aser—titasher)." R. Yochanan saw the young son of R. Shimon ben Lakish. He said to him: "Tell me what verse you learned in school." He said to him: "You shall surely tithe." He said to him "Tithe so that you will be rich." He said to him: "Is it permitted to test the Holy One, Blessed be He? Doesn't it say 'You should not test the Lord, your God'?" He said to him: "That is what R. Oshaya said: Except for this, for it says, 'Test me with this, said the Lord of Hosts, [and see if] I will not open for you the Heavens and rain down on you blessing *ad bli dai.*' What is ad bli dai? Rami bar Chama said that Rav said 'Until your lips will be tired (*yiblu*) from saying "enough!" (*dai*).' We learn that a person is commanded to tithe his money, and the more he gives [as part of the] tithes, the richer he gets. And whoever gives charity more than the tithes, the better, as long as he does not spend more than a fifth.[24]

Like R. Isaac of Vienna, his student, the Maharam of Rothenburg, related to the monetary tithe as a widespread custom:

> It would seem that after the tithe-monies were set aside for the poor, they should not be used for fulfilling a different commandment, for it looks like he is stealing from the poor, for even though it (the money tithe) is not from the Torah, but rather a custom, we have a standing principle that things that are permitted, and others consider them forbidden, you are not permitted to allow them in their presence, for it says "He should not profane his words." And that is a Rabbinical law, as it says in [Nedarim] 15a. And it is not like the case brought at the beginning of the first chapter of Arachin (6b): a Jew who committed himself to donate a candle and a lamp to a synagogue, it is permitted to use it for fulfilling a different commandment; for that case is different, for in both cases it is a deed done for the High (for God), but the poor have already merited the tithe money by custom, for the entire exile

has this custom, and one may not change [the usage] from [charity for] the poor to a different commandment for which the poor have no need, as it says in the second chapter of Shekalim (mishnah 5)—the remnants of the poor go to the poor.[25]

The Maharam relates to the custom of giving the tithe of the profits to charity as a custom and not as a commandment whose source is in the Torah or in the Rabbinical tradition. The custom creates an inferred stipulation, for the assumption is that anyone who sets aside money for a tithe intended it for charity alone. This assumption obligates the collectors to relate to this money as money intended only for charity.

The tension between this personal commandment and the public one can be explained by two Talmudic principles. According to one, charity is a personal commandment—one's obligation to care for the needs of one's relatives first. This principle is learned from the commandment of lending money, where it says: "Your poor and your town's poor—your poor come first. The poor of your town and the poor of another town—the poor of your town come first."[26] This obligation does not negate, of course, the individual obligation toward the poor of his own town, but by placing the position of a person's close relatives above that of other needy people it weakens the ability to raise enough money for the town's poor who have no relatives.

Indeed, against this principle of "your poor come first" we have R. Abba bar Zevda's saying in the Talmud: "Whoever gives his gifts to one priest, brings famine to the world."[27] This saying expresses the Sages' fear of denying the distant poor person his part and recommends balancing the principle of "your poor come first" by giving part of the charity to more distant poor people—those of the town at large. However, in the Talmud itself, I did not find an opinion that provides a balance between these two principles.

The existence of two obligations toward the poor—the individual's and the community's—raises a problem. The individual strives to fulfill his obligation to others out of a feeling of personal involvement and prefers his relatives. The collectors who bear the public responsibility toward the town's needy, however, prefer an objective, fair distribution.

This problem is not limited to the question of charity. The relationship between the individual's freedom and the desire for centralized action is one of those problems that arise from the dynamic character of the public organism—a changing and developing entity—and from the awareness of its individual components. In spite of the value attributed to the community, Jewish law accepts the freedom of the individual as a value that must be preserved and guides us to restrain ourselves when coming to the activation of community values. It grants an individual freedom of action whenever this will not bring about a collapse in the public arena.

A balance between the poor who is a close relative and the other needy people does appear in the works of the codifiers of the Middle Ages. Maimonides, for instance, related to this issue when dealing with the question of the tithes, and ruled that when giving *ma'aser ani*—the tithe intended for the poor—one must divide it into two equal parts. Half should go to one's poor relative and the other half "to any poor person going by."[28]

The Rabbis' awareness of the tension between individual and community generally led to matters being settled *within* the community. The laws of charity, like many of the laws relating to the community, were worked out through an intercommunal discussion between the individuals and the community at large—determined by the customs as well as the needs of the public and the individuals' consent as the Re'em (Constantinople, 1450–1526) wrote:

> Since vows and pledges are dependent only on the will of the entire community or its majority, then vows and pledges have also become one of those things that belong to the community, such as city laws, enactments and decrees. And therefore, just like in matters of city laws and enactments we go by the majority opinion in the community, so it is right that in matters of vows and pledges we should follow the majority opinion in the community.[29]

The response of the Rabbis in the Middle Ages who ruled on questions regarding this matter reflect the various patterns of solutions used by the communities. Some ruled from a position that supported the idea of protecting the public, and some ruled from a position that was concerned for the liberty of the individuals. Those who supported the public's interests did so because of a pessimistic approach, fearing that too much freedom of the individual will endanger the public. Those who advocated protecting the individuals' right to donate as they saw fit were more optimistic. It seems that the pessimistic approach expressed a relatively extreme stance, whereas the optimistic approach became the mainstream in Jewish Law. Both, however, maintained the legal framework that protects the basic rights of both the individual and the community.

The discussion between the Rabbis in the Middle Ages was based on the interpretation of a law brought in the Tosefta, and, to a certain degree, on its various versions. The Tosefta is dealing with the way of distributing money for charity and the collectors' authority when it comes to this distribution. The Tosefta discusses a case in which someone pledged money for charity but did not specify which charity. The Tosefta's assumption is that the individual prefers giving to the poor of his own town, to giving to the poor of another town, and similarly, the collectors prefer to give to the poor of their own town. Therefore, in the case of an unspecific pledge, the assumption is that the donor wished to donate to the local poor. At the end of the section, the Tosefta declares that in the case where the money has already been handed over to the collectors, the authority lies with the collectors, and not with the donor:

> An individual, who pledged money to charity in his town, gives it to the poor of his town. In another town—he gives it to the poor of the other town.

The collectors that pledged charity in their town give it to the poor of that town. In a different town, they give it to the poor of the other town. Someone who pledged money to charity, and the collectors have not taken it yet, is permitted to change it (its usage) to another cause. Once the collectors have it, he is not permitted to change it to another cause, unless they agree.[30]

There is disagreement among the Rabbis regarding the ruling in the Tosefta that the individual has the authority to determine where the money will go as long as he still has it in his own hands—a disagreement arising from different versions of the text. It turns out that there is another version of the Tosefta, according to which the last section grants full authority to the collectors, from the minute the individual has made his pledge verbally: "Someone who pledged money to charity, and the collectors have not taken it yet, is not permitted to change [its use] to another cause, unless they agree."[31]

Anyone who has made a verbal pledge to give of his money to the poor has thereby relinquished his right to determine the cause toward which it will go, and the authority is placed in the hands of the collectors.

This difference between two extant versions was apparently the basis of the disagreement among the authorities of the Middle Ages. Among the Western European authorities, the Ritzba (R. Isaac son of R. Abraham of Dampier died in 1210)[32] and R. Isaac of Vienna (1180–1250) thought that the authority was in the hands of the collectors. As a general rule, he tended to side with the public against the individual and thought that usually it was permitted to force a person to give charity.[33] In a responsum to the heads of a community who demanded that they be authorized to distribute all donations for charity, he accepted their stance. He based himself on a passage in the Talmud that grants the leadership of a central community the authority to collect from adjacent communities.[34] He thought that this outstanding authority given to collectors over people not from their community indicates that the collectors have sole authority in the community itself, and therefore any donation to charity, of any individual in the town, should be given over to the collectors:

> R. Isaac, son of R. Abraham of blessed memory answered: It seems to me that if a person has a relative in the town, he is not permitted to give his charity only to his relative, but rather he should give it to the town's collectors and they will distribute it as is suitable to each and every one. For even people from a town who have gone to another town and it was decided that they must give charity, they do not bring it with them if there is a [local] town leadership, but it will be given to the town leadership, as it says in chapter *Bnei Ha'ir*, and even more so this one, for he is not permitted to separate himself from the core members of the town and its leaders. And it also says in the Tosefta in Megillah that someone who pledged money to charity, and the collectors have not taken it yet, [is permitted to change its use to another cause. Once the collectors have it,][35] he is not permitted to change it for another cause, unless they agree. From this we understand that it has to be

distributed according to the opinion of the collectors, and even more so, if his relative is not living in the town, then he is not permitted to give it to him, as it says there: An individual who pledged charity (to another town, in his town) gives it to the poor of his own town. But only if he decided upon charity with the townspeople, for he cannot change from what the townspeople think, as I explained. But an individual who donated charity on his own initiative, may give it [to anyone he wants to] as I explained.[36]

It seems that the manuscript version of the Ritzva's responsum was changed in order to make it compatible with the first manuscript of the Tosefta.[37] In any case, the obligation to give charity monies to the collectors of the community depends, according to the Ritzva, on the assumption that they will act in accordance with Jewish Law, and will give some of the money to the donor's relatives as well, according to their judgment. The right of the donor to set aside money for his relatives must be preserved: "But an individual who donated charity on his own initiative, may give it to anyone he wants to." This is, however, only as an addition to the sum that he has given the collectors. The Ritzva adds that the limitation placed on the freedom of the individual to decide where his donations are going to go arises from a municipal decision, in which the individual participated, and which he agreed to: "But only if he decided upon charity with the townspeople."[38] The Ritzva's opinion that power must be given to the collectors continues Rashi's approach, according to which the collectors may use charity donations to buy even mats for the synagogue.[39]

Other Halakhah authorities held that as long as the money pledged for charity has not reached the hands of the town leaders, the decision regarding the destination of the monies remains in the hands of the donor, and he may do with his money as he wishes. R. Isaac of Vienna, for instance, held that in general the community institutions do not have the authority to take over all the fundraising for charity in the community, and giving money to charity should remain in the hands of the individual. According to him, the ruling to give the poor-tithe primarily to relatives should be teaching us the law about the commandment of giving charity in general:

> And I see that this is a *a-fortiori*: If with the poor-tithe that the Torah granted to the poor, and the owner of the field must tithe, he may give it to his relatives, how much more so charity, which a person gives on his own initiative, that he may be allowed to give to his relatives—up to half the amount. And it seems to me that particularly if he set aside money for charity, for distribution among the town's poor or poor people in general, then he cannot give to his poor relatives, and it will be divided as decided by both opinions, either by half or by third and two thirds. But if he pledged charity money without specifying, and did not say at the time of the pledge that he wishes to distribute it among the town's poor and poor people in general, then it belongs to his poor relatives, for we assume that anyone giving charity is doing so with the Torah law in mind, and the Torah says that your poor come before other poor people. And moreover, since he is

wealthy, the livelihood of his poor relatives is not placed as an obligation on the local collector, but rather on him, as mentioned above. So we see that the charity is theirs.... So it seems to me.[40]

R. Isaac of Vienna holds that the relative receives the charity by default, and therefore, in any case of a donation to charity where the receiving cause was not stipulated, we can assume that the giver intended to give to his relatives and not to the town poor. Even if the giver stated explicitly that he wishes the donation to be given to the town poor, the collectors must distribute the monies according to the accepted compromises—half-and-half, or one-third versus two-thirds.

When settling the disagreements, the responsa range from recognizing the greater power of the public to recognizing the individuals' demands, but it seems that as a matter of course R. Isaac's ruling was the one that was accepted as law in later times.[41] In another place, his opinion is brought in similar words:

> And from this I learn that a person who made a vow to give charity may give it to his poor relatives, up to half of all that he vowed to give, and according the other opinion even two parts he may give to his relatives from the tithe (even two parts ...). And this is a a-fortiori assumption: If even the poor-tithe that the Torah said to give to poor people he can give it to his relatives, up to half or two parts, all the more so charity, that he gives on his own initiative; this is true if he set aside money for charity and said it was for the general poor but if he pledged charity without specifying at the time of the pledge whom he wishes to distribute it to, he may give it all to his poor relatives; and more, since he is wealthy, and the responsibility for the livelihood of his poor relatives is placed on him and not on the local collectors, as it says in chapter *R. Eliezer* in Nedarim. So the charity is his relatives', and therefore they take it. So it seems to me, Isaac the son of Moshe.[42]

This discussion of the compromise —half or one and two-thirds, is discussed as well in the Mishnah and in the Tosefta, and later on, in the Jerusalem Talmud: "This measure is stipulated for the Priests, Levites and Israelites alike. Should he desire to save aught, he can only retain half and give the other half away. If he has only a very small quantity, then he must place it before them and then divide it among themselves."[43]

According to this Mishnah, any person, if he is a priest, a Levite, or an Israelite is permitted to give half of the Maaser to a needy relative and the other half to a stranger. The Tosefta quotes this possibility as well but adds another opinion—to give to the relative two thirds.[44]

The various approaches of the authorities all recognized the social pact as a factor that lies at the base of the public decision, just as they recognized the obligation of the individual to be personally involved. The only limitations of the public decision are the limitations placed on it by Jewish Law, and these determine that the total sum given to charity may not exceed one-tenth of a person's possessions and profits (or one-fifth of them, for those who wish to give more than is necessary). It is from this sum only that every person is obligated to help his relatives. The public decision will have to apply, therefore, to a compromise within the framework of these ten percent, so that the individual will be able to fulfill his obligation to his relatives, and the public will fulfill its obligations to the town poor. The form of compromise achieved in each society gives its public welfare institutions their particular character.

ENFORCING THE GIVING OF CHARITY

An important legal basis in viewing welfare as part of the public jurisdiction is the ability to force people to give charity. The option to coerce appears already in the Talmud and is usually connected with performing a commandment—religious coercion, and not the coercion of legal values—that is, justice. While this idea appears in the Talmud, there are also hints to the difficulties involved in such coercion. The question arises whether one ought to coerce someone to give charity, because taking money by force from people is considered a negative trait. The Talmud rules, at the end of the discussion, that one may force charity giving only on wealthy people, and that this should not be utilized against those who are not wealthy, even though they, too, are obligated to give charity:

> Our Rabbis taught: The charity fund is collected by two persons [jointly] and distributed by three. It is collected by two, because any office conferring authority over the community must be filled by at least two persons. It must be distributed by three, on the analogy of money cases [which are tried by a Beth din of three]. Food for the soup kitchen is collected by three and distributed by three, since it is distributed as soon as it is collected. Food is distributed every day, the charity fund every Friday. The soup kitchen is for all comers, the charity fund for the poor of the town only. The townspeople, however, are at liberty to use the soup kitchen like the charity fund and vice versa, and to apply them to whatever purposes they choose. The townspeople are also at liberty to fix weights and measures, prices, and wages, and to inflict penalties for the infringement of their rules.
>
> The Master said above: "Any office conferring authority over the community must be filled by at least two persons." Whence is this rule derived?— R. Nahman said: Scripture says, and they shall take the gold etc. This shows that they were not to exercise authority over the community, but that they were to be trusted. This supports R. Hanina, for R. Hanina reported [with approval] the fact that Rabbi once appointed two brothers to supervise the charity fund. What authority is involved [in collecting for charity]?—As was stated by R. Nahman in the name of Rabbah b. Abbuha, because the collectors can take a pledge for a charity contribution even on the eve of Sabbath. Is that so? Is it not written, I will punish all that oppress them, even, said R. Isaac b. Samuel b. Martha in the name of Rab, the collectors for charity?—There is no contradiction. The one [Rab] speaks of a well-

to-do man, the other of a man who is not well-to-do; as, for instance, Raba compelled R. Nathan b. Ammi to contribute four hundred zuz for charity.[45]

The leniency regarding coercing charity giving is thus limited to wealthy people. The authorities of the Middle Ages differed among themselves in regard to this ruling. There were those who held that charity is a voluntary act, subject only to each individual's whims, and that one may not force it on people. They argued that when the Talmud talks of coercing, it means persuading. This approach was articulated in the name of R. Yosef Tov Elem (eleventh century):

> The Rav, R. Yosef, asked R. Isaac the son of Abraham about the charity that the townspeople decide upon and there are individuals who refuse to go along with the majority opinion. And I heard that Rabbeinu Shemaya wrote in the name of Rabbeinu Yosef Tov Elem, that one does not enforce the giving of charity, even for a commandment, for it says "Because due to this thing [Hashem] will bless you." And we have the ruling that any commandment that has its reward mentioned, the law courts below (i.e., in this world) are not obligated to uphold, and it depends only on the generosity of the heart and words of convictions.[46]

R. Yosef Tov Elem maintained that it is forbidden to coerce a person to give charity. This tradition was continued in the twelfth century by Rabbeinu Tam. Others held that it is possible to coerce a person to give charity, even though it is a positive commandment. So thought R. Isaac of Dampier:

> And if you say, it says in Chulin (110a,) any positive commandment whose reward is specified, the earthly court of law is not required to uphold it, and about charity it says "for you will open your hand to him" and it says "for because of this thing [the L-rd] will bless you" (Deuteronomy 15:10) and Rabbeinu Tam says that that coercion is with words, as in Ketubot 53a. And he further explained that here they accepted upon themselves that the collector will force them, and to R. Isaac from Dampier it seems that with charity they coerce because there is a negative commandment in it, for it says "You shall not harden your heart and you shall not close your etc." And to the Ritzva it seems that the fact that the judges are not required to uphold a positive commandment whose reward is specified—that is when one is not punished. And so it seems from the Jerusalem [Talmud], and that one from Chulin ibid, where he did not honor his father and they tied him up and he said to them, let him free. The interpretation of that is that you are not obligated to coerce him until he does it, like with other positive commandments, for if he said to him "make a *succah* and a *lulav* and he doesn't make them, he is beaten until death, as it says in chapter … (Ketubot 86b, and ibid).[47]

Rabbeinu Tam understood charity as something that is left to a man's heart to decide, and that neither society nor any other person has any say in it. R. Isaac, by contrast, held that one may coerce a person to give charity even though it is a good deed and not a monetary obligation. The Ritzva, who was the disciple of Rabbeinu Tam and the Ri, continued Rabbeinu Tam's approach, but he held that the community is permitted to coerce a person if it wishes to do so, even though it is not obligated to do so:

> And R. Isaac the son of Abraham said, regarding charity that the townspeople decide upon and there are individuals who refuse, and Rabbeinu Yosef wrote that they do not coerce regarding it because its reward is specified. It is good what he wrote. I did not know and I was happy with these words, for now I have found a great sage [saying] according to my own words.... But in any case they are obligated and yet not punished if they disobey, as Reish Lakish said, that they are not punished if they don't coerce him.[48]

The Ritzva's opinion is that charity is not one of the commandments that the society must force the individuals to perform, but he ruled that it is permitted to do so: "For if a person does not want to put [anything] into the charity fund, the townspeople may force him."[49] That is what his teacher, the Ri, thought, that there is nothing to prevent the society from forcing a person to give charity. It seems that he understood the coercion in the context of migdar milta, meaning recognition of the need to force certain religious and moral values on individuals, even not in keeping with the strict law, in order to uphold the entire Torah.[50] It seems that the Ritzva, as well, saw the optional coercion in the same context, and therefore he equated the coercion to give charity with the conscientious coercion of the commandment of honoring one's parents.

The Maharam of Rotenburg clarified the issue and held that charity is a communal obligation, and the community is permitted to collect charity together with other communal taxes. This permission, and its connection to other communal taxes, makes one think that charity is a monetary obligation, an obligation concerning one's possessions:

> About Reuven who is separating himself from the community by not donating to the charity fund, and not paying taxes with them, if that was the custom in the town in the past, not to give together, but everyone gives by himself, they cannot force him and change their custom if he does not agree. But if the custom was to give together, he cannot separate himself from them, for we know from Chapter ... (Bava Batra 116b) that a partner cannot divide against the will of [the other] partner, and like in this case. It also seems so from [Chapter] ... (105a), and even if it is a new city, where there was no custom, it seems that he may be forced to give with them, to give into the fund, as it says in the Tosefta (Bava Metzia chapter 11): Townspeople coerce each other to build a synagogue and to buy them a Torah scroll, Prophets and the Writings and the same is with taking in guests and giving them charity, and so it seems from the first chapter of Bava Batra (8a): How long should he be in the town and be like the people of the town? Thirty

days for the soup kitchen, three months for the [charity] fund, six months to cover etc. So when someone comes to live [in a city] he is forced to give with them to charitable causes even though he never participated with them before. Peace will be upon you, Meir the son of R. Baruch.[51]

On the one hand, the Maharam argues that one cannot coerce another to give charity; yet he also says that the community's authority to take enables it to collect a welfare tax as well, that is, charity. Is this a monetary obligation, according to the Maharam? It seems that the Maharam is speaking of enforcing communal values and not pure legal-economic obligations. This communal obligation becomes a monetary obligation placed on each individual as an outcome of this communal obligation. The reason for this is that the communal obligation becomes an inferred stipulation because of which we assume that each and every individual accepts this obligation upon himself because he is living a communal life together with the other members of the community.

Among the Spanish Rabbis, it seems that there was mutual agreement regarding the community's authority to enforce charity giving on its members. They did not view the coercion as a legal one but as a moral and/or religious one. Maimonides, for instance, stated that:

He who does not want to give charity, or who gives less than is fitting for him, the court coerces him and beats him lashes, until he gives what they estimated for him to give. And they take from his possessions in his presence what is fitting for him to give. And collateral is taken for charity, even on the eves of the Sabbaths.[52]

The precise form of the coercion—lashes—indicates that this is not an action against one's possessions, but it is, rather, against the fault in his religious and moral behavior. The coercion is not seen in any way as a legal action similar to the action of collecting a debt—that is seen as a legal obligation, backed by a claimant. The obligation to give charity as described in the words of these Sages is a personal deed—"what is fitting for him"—and it arises from one's responsibility toward a needy person, not from his right to be helped. The claimants are community representatives—the collectors—not the needy person. The sanctions involved—lashes—points to the "educational" goals of the tradition of enforcing the performance of the commandments. The actual discussion of charity, starting from the point of obligation—of both the individual and the community—and not from the rights of the needy themselves, points to a paternalistic and nonegalitarian approach to the needy.

Nachmanides (Ramban also agreed with Maimonides' opinion)[53] holds that the coercion mentioned is not a fixed tax but a collection that the officials take upon themselves to collect for the sake of the needy. They coerce it in order to force the wealthy to fulfill their religious obligation but not to fulfill the right of the needy.

The Rashba (1235–1310), it seems, held that it is forbidden to take charity monies by force:

> You asked: [There is] a poor person, who has a wealthy father who does not want to support him financially, [claiming] that he is not obligated to support him, but rather as [he would] the other people of the town. May one coerce him in the court?
>
> Answer: As long as the children are very small—up to six [years], he must support them, and he is coerced to do so, and even if he is not well-off.... Beyond [age] six, as long as they are small, and are not capable of working, he is coerced orally (= persuasion).... And if he is well-off, he is coerced.... And it seems to me, that even if one has an adult child, if he (the father) is well-off, he is coerced to support him due to [the commandment to give] charity as in the case of Rava, and he is coerced to give charity more than the other rich men in town, and before they give, for he is obligated to support him due to the verse "And your brother will live with you" (Leviticus 25:36). And he cannot escape this obligation and say that he will support him together with the other rich men, through the charity collectors, for whoever falls [into poverty] does not fall first in the hands of the collector.[54]

The Rashba repeats the ruling that every father must support his children until they are six years old, as a basic obligation of a person toward his children. An additional obligation is one based on the commandment of giving charity, but in this case his obligation comes before that of the other town inhabitants, apparently according to the principle of "Your poor come first." The Rashba also repeats Rabbeinu Tam's claim that the coercion involved is merely oral—apparently even when we are talking about a wealthy person. The Rashba—like the other Rabbis I have mentioned—maintained that the coercion is not a legal obligation but a religious one having to do not with the rich person's possessions but with his conscience.

In another place, the Rashba based his ruling on the rulings of R. Hai Gaon, that one may not coerce a person to give charity if he is not present. R. Hay Gaon wrote in a responsum that even if a man vows, and he has an obligation to fulfill his vow within a year, the officials cannot coerce him to do so (such is the status of charity).[55]

According to the Rashba, coercion in matters of charity is taken to mean persuasion alone, and even that is limited to the case of a wealthy person who is standing in front of us. One may not force a person who is not wealthy or even persuade him, and one may not collect it from him unless he is physically present at the time. Against this stance of the Rashba, Rabbeinu Nissim Gerondi (The Ran; 1320–1380) said that there is nothing stopping the community from forcing one to give charity and to even requisition possessions for that purpose, whether the owner is there or not:

> And I am puzzled how he (the Rashba) wrote that one may not collect from a person's possessions even when the person is standing in front of us? For it says above, that if someone becomes insane, the court may requisition his possessions and support his wife.... And if that is so, that even in his presence his possessions are not requisitioned for the purposes of charity, certainly when he is not present, even though that he may leave without notice, so it seems certain that for charity one may requisition his possessions in his presence.[56]

Rabbeinu Nissim concludes from the ruling regarding a person who has become insane that the court is allowed to take charity from a person's possessions, for if that is so with an insane person, how much more so that it should be so with a person who is not insane. Significantly, the Ran's opinion was later accepted as the valid ruling.[57]

In any case, the differential coercion that arises from all these opinions points toward the focus as being on the person who is giving—the benefactor—rather than his money. The commandment to give charity was not intended to appease the poor person but to raise him out of his misery. It focuses on the poor person and on the benefactor who gives him of his money: on the poor person, according to his needs and degree of distress, and on the benefactor according to his available means.[58] In the end, charity is viewed as a religious commandment more than as a social or legal one. Through charity, the element of divine loving-kindness in man is actualized, more than through any other commandment. The Talmudic dictum expresses this well: "Rabbi Elazar said: the reword for charity is according to goodness, as it is said: "Sow righteousness for yourselves; Reap the fruits of goodness" (Hosea 10:12).[59]

As I have shown so far, coercing one to give charity was not viewed in any way as a legal action bearing the same meaning as collecting a loan in Jewish Law—which is viewed as a legal obligation, with a rightful claim being made by another person,[60] but as a coercion of the subject to fulfill a commandment. When we speak of a legal obligation, the coercion occurs within the framework of the relationship between two opponents. When talking about a religious commandment such as charity, the coercion is in an individual context, despite the fact that another individual stands to benefit from it.

Against my claim that charity is a religious commandment, we have a passage in the Talmud from which there seems to arise a real monetary obligation:

> Rav Chisda said in the name of Mar Ukva: Someone who has become insane, the court requisitions his possessions, and feeds and supports his wife and sons and daughters etc.... What is etc? Says Rav Chisda: that is jewelry. Rav Yosef said: Charity. The one who said jewelry, even more so charity; the one who said charity, but jewelry is given to her, because he would not want his wife to be unadorned.[61]

In a case where a person has lost his sanity and his judgment, the court appoints a guardian who takes care of his spiritual and material needs. According to the Tosafot, the case is of one who has become insane after having accumulated possessions and supported his family and given of his money to charity.[62] This ruling appears already in Maimonides' code:

> The guardians provide the young children with a *lulav* and a *succah* and *tzitzit* and a shofar and a Torah scroll, *tefillin* (phylacteries) and mezuzah and a [Purim] megillah. The rule is: any positive commandment that has a limit, whether it is a Torah commandment or a Rabbinical one, [the guardian] provides, even though they are not obligated in any commandment (yet), but [are doing it] only in order to educate them. But they do not take charity from them, even for the ransom of captives, because these commandments have no limit. And someone who became insane or deaf, the court takes charity from him, if he is worthy.[63]

Maimonides assumes that the insane and the deaf are both obligated to give charity. Yet, he differentiates between the obligations of a orphan's guardian, who is not allowed to take from their money and give it to charity, and the obligations of an insane or deaf person's guardian—he is told to take of their money and give it charity, even though the insane person is exempt from all Torah commandments.[64] It should be noted that Maimonides was careful to say "someone who became insane" and not "the insane." Maimonides is not relating to people who were congenitally mentally unbalanced or deaf, but to people who were sane, but then lost their sanity.[65] Just as in the case of someone who became rich and later left his house and emigrated to another country (in which case the court requisitions his possessions in order to support his family), so, too, here in the case of someone who became wealthy but then became insane.[66] From this standpoint, we can explain Maimonides' words as saying that the court of law is assuming knowledge of the true intentions of the person who lost his sanity or his hearing—that if he were still sane and hearing he would wish to give charity. R. Yosef Karo explained Maimonides thus: "*Rabbeinu*'s reason is that it can be assumed that any person would be pleased to give charity from his money."

Based on the assumption that a person would wish to give charity, we assume that one who has lost his sanity wanted, when he was still sane, to give charity, and therefore, while he is insane, we do his will and take charity from his possessions. But R. Yosef Karo added another explanation: "for a person's money is subjugated, to give charity from it."[67] This statement seems to leave no room for doubt that charity is a legal obligation placed on a person's possessions, and subjugates them. According to R. Efraim Navon (1677–1735), in his book *Machaneh Efraim*, the subjugation applies only to someone who pledged charity when he was still sane—whether explicitly or implicitly. When asked why charity is taken from an insane person, who is exempt from all the commandments, he, too, concluded that the case is of one who lost his sanity and not of someone born mentally unstable:

> Seemingly one should ask regarding an insane person, since the obligation of fulfilling the commandment is placed on him—but he is exempt from all the commandments, so how can subjugation of possessions be relevant here? For this obligation is not like other, regular monetary obligations. For if he owed a *maneh* (a sum of money) to Reuven, it is taken from him, even after he became insane, for this is different, for he became obligated when he was still well ... but to obligate him after he has become insane with coming [payments for] livelihood, since he has not yet become obligated in them, and there is no obligation upon him to fulfill a commandment now, we can also conclude that the court of law does not take it from his possessions, and we must say that the reason for this here is because we assume that he would want to support his children.[68]

According to the Machaneh Efraim, the basic assumption is that a person wants to support his children and give charity, and therefore even when he has lost his sanity, the court of law Din can collect charity from his possessions.

In the nineteenth century, a dispute arose about this topic. R. Aryeh Leib Heller (known as the Ketzot Hachoshen, 1745–1812) thought that the subjugating of possessions mentioned in the *Kesef Mishneh* means a real monetary obligation that the owner has toward the poor: "the money of the poor people is for him as if he owes them a real debt, so the fact that we force him is actually [an act of] returning to the poor what he owes them."[69] However, R. Yaakov Lorberbaum of Lisa (1770–1832), author of the *Netivot Mishpat*, opposed this opinion of the Ketzot Hachoshen and said that the subjugation of one's money to charity as mentioned in the Kesef Mishneh applies to possessions whose owner pledged charity from them in the past. When the owner did not state ahead of time that he wishes to give charity, there is no subjugation of property:

> See the Ketzot Hachoshen, who proved that there is subjugation of possessions when it comes to charity. And according to my humble opinion, it seems that there is no subjugation of possessions, unless it is a case the court of law may enforce charity giving by law, such as in order to support a relative, or give to the communal charity treasury and to the town's soup kitchen, for these obligations came upon him not from the power of his speech. But an obligation that comes from [his] power of speech is like a vow, and there is not subjugation of possessions.[70]

Only an explicit statement of intention to donate money to charity creates a subjugation of possessions and enables the collection of the amount from the possessions, if the intention was not carried out. This ruling gets support from the fact that Maimonides' ruling applies only to one who has become insane, and not to one who was born insane. Regarding the latter, Maimonidesis also holds that he is exempt from giving charity.

COERCION AND RIVALRY

As illustrated, there is indeed the concept of coercing one to give charity in the Talmudic law in certain situations, but it is not a legal coercion in the same sense of coercing someone to repay a loan or to pay for something he purchased. This claim has many ramifications for many laws, among others on the father's obligation to support his young children.[71] Regarding this issue, there have been contradicting arguments. There are those who claim that the obligation to support children, based on the laws of charity, constitutes a debt, creating rivalry between the father and his children. R. Simcha Kaplan claimed, for instance, that charity is a legal obligation and not simply a moral one:

> It seems clear that the law that one coerces the giving of charity does not come from the law that one is coerced to fulfill the commandments; for in the law of enforcing the commandments we have not found that [sums] are collected from his possessions. It is only that the court of law has the obligation to coerce [a person] to fulfill the commandment, and since Maimonides thinks that with charity the court of law coerces [a person] and also collects from his possessions, we see from this that it is a special law regarding coercion to give charity.[72]

The coercion of collecting from possessions proves, according to R. Kaplan, that we are dealing with a debt that is placed on the possessions, and not on a person's obligation to perform his religious and moral obligations. One may conclude from him that it is a monetary obligation of the rich person, with the poor person having a "monetary claim" against him.[73] Opposed to R. Kaplan's opinion, a Rabbinical court consisting of Rabbis Goldschmidt, Karelitz, and Babliki ruled that the obligation to give charity is an obligation placed on the donor, with no parallel right of the needy. In other words, this is an obligation that does not create the rivalry of claimant and/or defendant, between the needy person and the donor:

> If the obligation is because of the enactment [obligating one to] support [one's children], the enactment is that a father must provide his child with food, meaning that the father owes something to his child. But if the obligation comes from charity, the person who was told to give charity must give, but it is an obligation that relates to him; he does not owe it to the receiver, meaning, the receiver does not have a debt by him. And even if the receiver is a person that the one obligated to give is especially obligated to give him charity, such as a father to his child, as explained, this does not mean that the father owes a monetary debt to the child, but rather the father is obligated in general to give charity … without there being any debtee that he owes him, and in this general obligation there are priorities as to whom one should give, and who are the first in line for collection, and according to this order, the father comes first regarding his child, as opposed to another person, and the father is told to give his son more than

the other people who are obligated to give. But he does not owe a debt to his son. Although the Radbaz, in his commentary on Maimonides ... "and it is like a debt upon him and he is coerced to pay off his debt and it is collected from his possessions...." But this does not contradict what we have said, for even though the debt of charity is like any other debt, it is a general one, that the person from whom it is requested is obligated to pay, but it is not a direct debt that the person from whom it is requested owes towards an individual ... but if the obligation is due to a Rabbinical enactment, he does owe a debt to his child, and it is like any other debt, where the person owing is a defendant opposing the claimant—the person to whom it is owed, and therefore it is his power to admit.[74]

According to the court's ruling, the obligation of a father toward his children is dependent on its definition: Is it the obligation to support children, or is it charity? An enactment creates a monetary obligation of the father toward his child, in which there is rivalry. Once there is rivalry, the child is permitted to sue his or her father, in order to collect what is owed. If the father's obligation to his child is based on fulfilling the commandment to give charity, the obligation placed on the father is a personal obligation that does not create rivalry, and this means that the child may not sue the father. Enforcing the support of children, in this case, is the community's responsibility, and the litigation will be between the father and the community, and not the father and the child.

Coercion does have an important role in any judiciary system, but it is not the substance of the judicial process. Jewish law does not view this matter as a question of positive law (according to which the judgment is the result of laws made by a body whose right to do so is deemed to be derived from the fact that it has the power to do so). The Talmudic law is divided into several realms; in each one, there are different rules regarding evidence and judicial frameworks. According to this outlook, Deve Rabbi Yanai promised a person who swallows his pride when being insulted the reward of being able to differentiate between monetary issues and capital-punishment issues: "Any student whose teacher gets angry at him once and twice and remains silent—merits to differentiate between monetary and capital-punishment issues."[75]

Coercion on its own does not characterize any one of the realms. The differentiation is the result of a conglomeration of definitions.[76] Coercing the giving of charity is a coercion to perform a moral deed. This deed might be done together with others as a commandment that applies to all community members; in this situation, a person can be coerced to give, but in no way is it defined as a debt that the individual owes to his needy fellow man, but as a commandment that obligates anyone who has the means and helps the unfortunate.

The obligation to demand from the individual to give charity is placed on the community, and is based on the commandment of "You shall surely rebuke your fellow."[77] It is placed on any person according to his ability, and changes accordingly. Every individual is commanded to rebuke his fellow Jew, but he must do it in a way that will not create discord. However, when we are dealing with an authoritative body, it has an even greater obligation to rebuke. Therefore, the court is obligated to make enactments and punish according to the present needs: "A court should flog someone who has not merited flogging and kill one who has not merited being killed—and not as a transgression of Torah but in order to create a fence for the Torah."[78] This obligation is placed even on a king of Israel[79] and on any political authority.

DISTRIBUTIVE JUSTICE

One may coerce a person to give charity, and charity is a commandment that obligates the community as well. The question is if this phenomenon can be defined as distributive justice, in the sense it is used in modern judicial thought. It seems to me that this is not the case.

The public domain is defined, first of all, as one that serves the property rights of the individuals, and justice does not suggest redistribution but rather protection of these property rights. Moreover, the commandment to give charity does not seek to undermine the right to own property, and certainly one does not see in it the demand to redefine the right of property or even to curtail it.

These two phenomena—property rights and charity—are both based on a single theological principle: Man was created in the image of God. Man is seen as bearing divine qualities "a part of God from Above"[80] and as someone whom God sees as having a covenantal relationship with him even after he left the Garden of Eden. Just as God rules the world, so he gives man a status of sovereignty and freedom in the world and commands him: "and rule over the fish of the sea and the birds of the sky."[81]

Man's liberty expresses itself in acts of will; in controlling the world and adapting it to man's spirit. Man's control of the world, when realized in accordance with the laws of the Torah, does not contradict the Creator's sovereignty; indeed, it even constitutes an application of the covenant between them. The divine element in man consists not only in being a free ruler of himself. In man's quality of rulership, there is also a sympathetic connection to the world, similar to the love and concern that the Holy One, blessed be he, shows toward creation, as expressed in the *midrash*:

> When the Holy One, Blessed be He, created the First Man, he took him and went by all the trees in the Garden of Eden, and said to him: See My creations, how attractive and fine they are, and everything I created, I created for you. Make sure not to ruin and destroy My world, for if you ruin [it], there is no one who can fix [it] after you.[82]

God relates to the world with loving-kindness and mercy, in spite of his being transcendental and independent of it. This combination of relating and separateness exists in man too. In every person there is an autonomous element, unique and different from his fellow man. At the same time, man is an emotional creature who has a sense of closeness to the world and to other people. This combination is the divine quality of man, and it is from it that his characteristic as a ruler but also as a bearer of responsibility arises. It is the quality that makes him a partner in the covenant with God. What we learn from this is that man's ownership of property has a value in itself, and therefore man's rulership is expressed, according to Jewish Law, in ownership. Man also bears a responsibility toward other people, one that is expressed in the concept of *chessed* (helping others). The covenant that God makes with man is not between equals but between an authoritative figure and his subjects. God rules the heavens and man rules the earth, as the verse says, "The heavens are heavens for Hashem, and the earth he gave to human beings."[83] The source of authority in the world is God, who shared his authority with man. Even if man was created in the image of God, he is still an earthly creature, subject to God and his authority. Man is not given the opportunity to compete with God, and therefore the Torah guides him toward realizing his divine qualities in a normative framework and limits his liberty in the context of honoring God and his commandments.[84]

The aspiration to combine the obligation to give charity with the right to own property in a way that redefines the right to own property bases itself on a systemic stance that wishes to find solutions within the system—to create an autarchic system that will not need human judgment. That is, however, not the way of Talmudic law. As Chaninah ben Menachem showed, Talmudic law is in the hands of people, whereas the classical Western approach is that the law is in the hands of the rulers.[85] In Talmudic law, which is in the hands of people, the reining-in of egotism is not done by balancing the system. The problem of poverty will thus not be solved by a systemic redistribution of the wealth but rather by encouraging, caring, and giving to others. Therefore, one must not confuse charity with concepts of justice. This is a moral commandment that applies to human beings, and they are made responsible to their fellow people. Society as a whole bears the responsibility of encouraging the individuals to give from their money to charity, and even to force them to fulfill this commandment—but not to take the money and redistribute it.

CONCLUSION

An unanswered question thus far is whether the social obligations articulated in the Jewish tradition translate into support for a generous welfare state. Based on the reading of Jewish tradition outlined above, it may be argued that a state should bear some responsibility and help the needy—but it is a responsibility that functions from the bottom up rather than from the top down. While the state does have particular welfare responsibilities, these should supplant the primary responsibility that falls on the individual and families. How such concrete responsibilities on the part of individuals are actualized is the subject of the next chapter.

NOTES

1. Zeev Falk, *Erchei Mishpat Veyahadut: Likrat philosophia shel hahalacha* (Jerusalem, 1980), 117, 119; Chanoch Dagan, "Dinei Asiyat Osher: Bein yahadut leliberalism," in *Mishpat Vehistoria*, ed. Daniel Gottwin and Menachem Mautner (Jerusalem, 1999), 178–90; Shimon Federbush, *Mishpat Hamelucha Beyisrael* (Jerusalem, 1952), 23–25, 126–28, 138–40; Rabbi Aharon Lichtenstein, "Leveirur 'Cofin al Midat Sedom,'" in *Hagut Ivrit BeAmerica*, ed. Menachem Zohari, Aryeh Tartakover, and Chaim Ormian (Tel Aviv, 1972), 380–81; Meir Tamari, *With All Your Possessions* (Jerusalem, 1998), 36–38, 52–56, 210–11, 240, 242–43, 248–49, 277; Ephraim Frisch, *An Historical Survey of Jewish Philanthropy* (New York, 1924), 77, 80; Michel Walzer, *Spheres of Justice: A Defense of Pluralism and Equality* (New York, 1983), 3–6, 75–778, 92.

2. Tamari, 37–38; Menachem Ben Shalom, *Hasids and Hasidism in the Periods of the Second Temple and the Mishna* (Tel Aviv, 1998), 52–53.

3. Lichtenstein, 362–80; Dagan, 179.

4. Lichtenstein, 380–81.

5. Federbush, 126–27.

6. Kister, "Dinei Tzedakah Beshimusham Bamishpat BeYisrael," in *Hapraklit*, vol. 24, 168–69.

7. Frisch, 77. Frisch was the first to point out the etymological connection between *tzedaka* (charity) and *tzadikut* (righteousness); according to him, it arises from the changing meanings between biblical and Talmudic language. In the Bible, *tzedaka* means *tzadikut*, in other words, the characteristic of a righteous person, whereas in the language of the Talmudic Sages, it means giving money to the needy. See also Tamari, 36: "The Divine origin of wealth is the central principle of Jewish economic philosophy. All wealth belongs to God, who has given it temporarily to man, on the basis of stewardship, for his physical wellbeing," 52: "The 'haves' in Judaism have an obligation to share their property with the 'have nots,' since it was given to them by God partly for that purpose." See below, note 64.

8. Tamari, p. 52: "Charity is not simply an act of kindness but rather the fulfillment of a legal obligation"; p. 240: "The community has a responsibility for the welfare of its members and a corresponding right to finance those needs through taxation over and above the individual's duty to contribute to charity." See also page 277. Public responsibility does not allow the public to collect more than the amount that an individual is obligated for because this is not a legal obligation. The community is allowed to oversee only the distribution (see more on this below). See also Dagan, p. 179:

    The giving of charity in Jewish tradition is not a matter of mercy, kindness, generosity or personal conscience, but rather a matter of justice (thus explaining the linguistic affinity between *tzedakah* and *tzedek*). Giving charity is a fulfillment of a legal obligation: the realization of the community's rights and the rights of the unfortunates in the community, by way of the possessions of those who have.

Dagan's main claim is based on a Talmudic discussion regarding a person who benefits from another's resources, while not depleting them in any way; in his opinion, this principle is a result of the ruling that a person is forced to give if it does not harm him ("coercion over the trait of Sodom"). The problem with this claim is that according to most medieval scholars—and their opinion was accepted as the common ruling—there is no connection between benefit without any obligation attached and the coercion over the trait of Sodom. Therefore, his assumption that it is possible to force a rich person to give of his possessions to the poor person is mistaken. According to Dagan, only some loss that the poor person causes the rich can absolve the rich man from the legal obligation of benefitting the poor. However, according to Jewish Law, the virtual interactions that take place between the receiver and the giver who does not lose anything in the process are contractual and based on the benefit. The minute the benefit causes loss, the virtual contract translates into a legal claim against the one who has benefitted. Only a benefit that does not cause loss does not create a contractual obligation and does not entail any claim for payment.

9. Walzer, 3–6, 75–78, 92.

10. Mishnah, Avot 5:1: "There are four character types among people. He who says what is mine is mine and what is yours is yours is an average character; some say it is the character of Sodom (*middat Sodom*)."

11. Maimonides, *Mishneh Torah, Hilchot Matnon Aniyim* 10:2, and see 10:1 as well.

12. *BT*, Yevamot 14a. The beginning of the verse is "You are children of the L-rd your God" (Deut. 14:1).

13. See Responsa of the Maharam of Rothenburg (Lemberg/Levov), 108.

14. Mishnah, Demai 3:1; Kiddushin 4:5; Bava Kamma 10:1.

15. Tosefta, Peah 4:15; Demai 3:16–17; Bava Kamma 11:6; Bava Metzia 3:9.

16. *BT*, Sanhedrin 17b. The records of Jewish communities in Europe indicate the wide prevalence of the charity collectors. See, for example, *Pinkas Kahal Tiktin 5301–5566*, ed. Mordechai Nadav (Jerusalem, 1997), sec. 242, 152.

17. *BT*, Bava Batra 8b.

18. Maimonides, *Mishneh Torah, Hilchot Matnot Aniyim*, 9:5.

19. Mishnah, Kiddushin 4:5; *BT*, Bava Batra 8a–9b.

20. Maimonides, *Hilchot Matnon Aniyim* 9:3.

21. Tosafot, Ta'anit 9a, "*Aser Te'aser*." For a thorough study of the custom of monetary-tithe see Judah Galinski, "Custom, Ordinance or Commandment? The Evolution of the Medieval Monetary-Tithe in Ashkenaz" *Journal of Jewish Studies*, vol. 62, no. 2 (Autumn 2011): 203–32.

22. *Pesikta Derav Kahana*, ed. by Dov, son of Yaakov Yisrael Mandelbaum, sec. 10, vol. a (New York, 1952), 172.

23. See *Sefer Chassidim* (Bologne Manuscript), 144.

24. R. Isaac, son of R. Moshe of Vienna, *Sefer Or Zarua*, Zhitomir, 1852, pt. 1, Laws of Charity, 13.

25. Responsa of the Maharam of Rothenburg (Prague), 74: "The money of the tithe, it seems that if they were intended to be given to the poor, they should not be used for [fulfilling] a different commandment"; Responsa of the Maharam of Rothenburg, Munich manuscript, 338; 75: "And to give out his tithes [to his] big [children]." Also, see Rema, Shulchan Aruch Yoreh Deah 349:1, and the Shach there, 3.

26. *BT*, Bava Metzia 72a. This rule was said originally in reference to lending money to a poor person.

27. *BT*, Eiruvin 63a.

28. Maimonides, *Mishneh Torah, Hilchot Matnot Aniyim* 6:11. R. Isaac son of R. Moshe of Vienna, *Or Zarua*, pt. 1, Laws of Charity, 22; see also Mishnah Peah 8:6. On the other hand, see Tosefta (Liberman Edition), Peah 4:2: "Abba Yoseh son of Dustai said in the name of R. Liezer: If he wants, he places a third before them, and leaves two parts to his relatives." This is the ruling that was later accepted. See, for instance, R. Yechiel Michel Epstein, *Aruch Hashulchan*, Yoreh Deah 251:5:

    The man who makes a living like an important person, who eats well—bread and meat and cooked foods—and is dressed and covered properly, certainly is obligated to give charity—one tenth or one fifth of his livelihood [for if he does not have a sufficient livelihood he should not be obligated even this sum] and a great part of the charity he should give to his relatives and the town poor, and a small amount he is obligated to give to far away people and to the poor of another town, for otherwise [in] a town of poor people they will starve to death, God forbid.

29. Responsa of R. Eliyahu Mizrachi (the Re'em), 53. See Shach, Shulchan Aruch Yoreh Deah, 251:9.

30. Tosefta Megilla (Lieberman) 2:15. And in a similar version of that, in the London Manuscript:

    An individual who pledged money for charity in his town, gives it to the people of his town. Elders who pledged in their city give it to the poor of that city. One who pledges money for charity, as long as the elders have not taken it, they are allowed to change [its use] to something else. Once the elders have taken it, he may not change [its use] to something else, unless they agree.

    Also in the JT, Megillah 3:2, and Nachmanides in his *chiddushim*, Bava Batra 8b.

31. Tosefta (Liberman), Megillah 2:15, according to the Erfurt manuscript. And this same version appears in the Responsa of the Rashba (Jerusalem, 1997), pt. 1, 604.

32. Efraim A. Auerbach, *Ba'alei Hatosafot* (Jerusalem, 1976), 270, n. 47. The Ritzba was French, but for the purpose of this discussion one should consider northern France and Germany as one unit. See, for instance, Chaim Soloveitchik, *Yeinam* (Tel Aviv, 2003), 17–18.

33. *Sefer Or Zarua*, pt. 1, Laws of Charity, 4. Tosafot, Bava Batra 8b, D'H Akfe.

34. *BT*, Megillah 27a–b.

35. This addition in parenthesis was not in the original printing of the Or Zarua, and was added on from the Savionita printing (1514 AD), according to the London manuscript of the Tosefta. But see Saul Lieberman, *Tosefta Kipeshuta*, pt. 5, 1156. According to him, the Tosefta that the Ritzba had was from the Erfurt manuscript, which lacked the addition in the parenthesis, and therefore the addition is a mistake.

36. R. Isaac son of R. Moshe of Vienna, *Sefer Or Zarua*, pt. 1, Laws of Charity, 23 (Zhitomir, 1852). See also Mordechai, Bava Batra, 502, and the Beit Yosef on Tur Yoreh Deah, 251.

37. See n. 28.

38. The Maharam of Rothenberg presented a similar claim in his Responsa, pt. 4 (Prague), 918: "About Reuven who is separating himself from the community by not donating to the charity fund and not to pay taxes with them, if the townspeople had this custom from long ago [not] to give together but each one gives on his own, they cannot coerce him and change their custom if he does not agree, but if they had the custom of giving together, he cannot separate himself from them."

39. See Bava Batra 8b, and Rashi, ibid.

40. R. Isaac son of R. Moshe of Vienna, *Sefer Or Zarua* (Zhitomir, 1852), pt. 1, Laws of Charity, 22. see also the Mordechai, Bava Batra, 500. In saying "It seems to me" the Or Zarua means to point to the fact that he does not agree with the Ritzva. In the Mordechai, on the other hand, the sentences are brought in a single continuum.

41. Shulchan Aruch and the Rema, Yoreh Deah, 251:5. See also the Beit Yosef, Tur Yoreh Deah 251:5; R. Eliezer of Metz, the Shita Mekubetzet Nedarim 65b, the Kol Bo 82, and the Tashbetz Hakatan 405, in the name of the Maharam of Rothenburg. The Ritzva's responsum was quoted with the addition of the words "he who separates money for charity" and that is the way it is mentioned in the context of trying to determine the intentions of someone who pledged money for charity but did not specify his intentions. See the Mordechai: "He who pledges money for charity and has a relative in town is not permitted to give it only to his relative, but rather should give it to the town charity collectors and they will distribute it properly to each and every one." Also see this quote in the Beit Yosef mentioned above.

42. R. Mordechai son of R. Hillel Hacohen, *Sefer Hamordechai*, Bava Batra, 659.

43. Mishnah, Peah 8:6.

44. Tosefta Peah (Lieberman Edition) 4:2, according to the Vienna Manuscript. See more *JT*, Peah 8:6.

45. *BT*, Bava Batra 8b.

46. Mordechai, Bava Batra, 490.

47. Tosafot, Bava Batra 8b. See also R. Isaac son of Isaac son of Moshe of Vienna, *Or Zarua*, pt. 1, Laws of Charity, 4 (Zhitomir, 1852). See also the Ran on Ketubot 18a; Nachmanides on Bava Batra 8b. About the Ritzba see Efraim A. Auerbach, *Ba'alei Hatosafot* (Jerusalem 1996), 261–71.

48. Ibid.

49. *Or Zarua*, pt. 1, Laws of Charity, 4.

50. *BT*, Yevamot 90b.

51. Responsa of the Maharam of Rothenburg, pt. 4 (Prague), 918.

52. Maimonides, *Mishneh Torah, Hilchot Matnon Aniyim* 7:10. And see more about coercing to perform commandments *Migdar Milta*, The court of law should flog.... Maimonides, *Mishneh Torah, Hilchot Sanhedrin* 24:4.

53. Nachmanides, *Chiddushei Harambam* on Bava Batra 8b.

54. R. Shmuel son of R. Avraham Ben Aderet, *Responsa of the Rashba* (Jerusalem, 1997), pt. 3, 292. See more there, pt. 4, 56.

55. R. Shmuel son of R. Avraham Ben Aderet, *Chiddushei Harashba* on Ketuvot 49b.

56. Rabbeinu Nissim on the Rif, Ketuvot 18a.

57. *Yam Shel Shlomo* on Ketuvot, chap. 4, 17: "And the main [opinion] that seems to me is the words of the Ran."

58. As in Maimonides, *Mishneh Torah, Hilchot Matnot Aniyim* 7:1: "It is a positive commandment to give charity to the poor as is suitable to the poor person, if the giver can afford it." Tamari's words on the matter are very different: "Tzedaka has the same root as 'Tzedek'—justice—since acts of assistance are looked upon in Jewish thought primarily as a reflection of a social imbalance. They are not merely prompted by mercy or personal pangs of conscience, but rather constitute the fulfillment of the obligations that flow from wealth," Tamari, 248. He bases this statement on Maimonides' words in his *Guide for the Perplexed*, but Maimonides himself defined the term *tzedek* completely differently. Regarding forcing the public to save the life of a needy person see *BT*, Gittin 45a. See *Pitchei Teshuva*, Yoreh Deah 254 for saving a person who is in a life-endangering situation.

59. *BT*, Succah 49b. For a contradicting opinion, see R. M. A. Amiel, Middot Lecheker Hahalacha, Middah 11, who claims that religious commandments have a social-legal dimension, based on the words of R. Shimon Shkop in Sha'arei Yosher 5:1.

60. In my opinion, Hoffeld's table is applicable only in the case of a legal debt and not in the case of a debt based on performing a religious commandment. This does not have power against an obligation.

61. *BT*, Ketubot 48a.

62. Tosafot, ibid. ‎ולא שאני לך.

63. Maimonides, *Mishneh Torah*, *Hilchot Nachalot* 11:10–11.

64. Maimonides, *Mishneh Torah*, *Hilchot Chagiga* 2:4.

65. The use of the verb *nishtateh* to describe someone who was mentally fit but then became mentally ill is used by Maimonides repeatedly. See *Hilchot Ishut* 12:17; 13:7; Hilchot Geirushin 2:17; 6:8. Hilchot Shoteh 1:10; Hilchot Shegagot 3:7; Hilchot Edut 14:2. In all those references, the person being described is married, and therefore it is clear that when he married his wife he was sane, for otherwise the marriage would not have been valid. In Hilchot Edut, it says explicitly that the person was sane and became insane. There is not even one case where the discussion is around someone who was born mentally ill.

66. Maimonides, Hilchot Ishut 12:16–17.

67. R. Yosef Karo, *Kesef Mishneh*, Hilchot Nachalot 11:11.

68. R. Efraim Navon, *Machaneh Efraim* Constantinople, 1738, Bnei Brak, 1986, Hichot Tzedakah 1. See also Shut Maharit, Part I, 127.

69. R. Aryeh Leib Heller, *Ketzot Hachoshen*, Choshen Mishpat 290, 3

70. R. Yaakov Lorberbaum, *Netivot Hamishpat*, Choshen Mishpat 290, 8.

71. See Menashe Shava, "*Mezonot Yeladim Ketinim: Hayachas bein techulat dinei hatzedek shebamishpat ha'ivri levein techulat chok letikun dinei mishpacha (Mezonot), 1959,*" *Dinei Yisrael* 4, 181–217.

72. R. Simcha Kaplan, "*Kefiyah Bitzedaka,*" *Kovetz Torani, Mazkeret lezecher Hagra Hertzog* (Jerusalem, 1952), 354.

73. Ibid., 355.

74. File no. 226/5714, פר"ד, Judges: R. Eliezer Goldschmidt, R. Shaul Karelitz, R. Y. Babliki, vol. 1, 154–55. See also Zerach Warhaftig's comment, "*Lemekorot Hachovah Lemezonot Yeladim,*" *Techumin* 1, 1980, 268.

75. *BT*, Brachot 63b.

76. See Menachem Elon, *Hamishpat Ha'ivri* (Jerusalem, 1984), 100–57, about religious, monetary, and moral law and about the interactions between them.

77. Leviticus 19:17.

78. Maimonides, Hilchot Sanhedrin 24:4.

79. Maimonides, Hilchot Melachim Umilchamot 4:10.

80. Job 31:2.

81. Genesis 1:28. This commandment was given to Adam while he was still in the garden of Eden but did not change even after the sin. See *BT*, Yevamot 65b; Kiddushin 35a.

82. Kohellet Rabba (Vilna), 7.

83. Psalms 115:16.

84. There are a few cases described in the Bible and in the *midrash* in which man com-
     peted, so-to-speak, with the Creator, and in all of them he failed. Adam was banished
     from the Garden of Eden so that he would not eat from the Tree of Life: "For man has
     been like one of us to know good and bad, and now he might send his hand and take
     also from the Tree of Life and eat and live forever" (Gen. 3:22). Similarly, the human
     attempt to build the Tower of Babel: "And the L-rd said, for they are one nation and
     one language they all have an ..." (Gen. 11:6).

85. Chanina Ben Menachem, "*Hamishpat Ha'ivri Vehamishtar Hachukati Bimedinat
     Yisrael*," *Masa el Hahalacha*, ed. Amichai Barholtz (Tel Aviv, 2003), 466–67. —*Judicial
     Deviation in Talmudic Law: Governed by Men, Not by Rules* (Princeton: Routledge,
     1990), 1. I have extended the scope of Chanina Ben Menachem's ideas, which relate
     originally to the role of the judge.

4

GENEROSITY

This chapter turns to consider charitable acts that do not involve the redistribution of property. Let us call these acts of *generosity*. Thus far we have approached economics from the legal and practical standpoints: if and how, for example, property should be distributed or whether governments have the right to regulate charity or even implement welfare measures.

One function of economic theory is to trace the vectors that push the market forward and to identify the motives that create an atmosphere of prosperity. In matters of competition, these motives are usually regarded as generally egocentric, composed of self-interest and envy. However, is this the full story? Can the market be motivated by the self-interest of individuals alone or are there other moral forces and values at play?

John D. Mueller has argued that Western economic thought has undergone two major revolutions. The first came about as a result of Thomas Aquinas' work, while the second was inaugurated by Adam Smith. Aquinas' theory was partly the outgrowth and synthesis of Aristotle's theory of distributive justice and Saint Augustine's moral idea of distribution. It does not see distribution as serving only egoistic purposes (or "non-altruism") such as selling and buying but includes gift giving as well. Following Aquinas' description, the market consists of four elements: production, exchange, distribution, and consumption.[1]

Adam Smith is best known for his analysis of the market as a self-correcting mechanism. His theory of pure economics has no place for charity, even though his moral theory as expressed in his *Theory of Moral Sentiments* certainly does.

Even distribution—because it no longer answered to a notion of distributive justice—ceased to carry. Thus the two elements with which Adam Smith is left are production and exchange.

Smith also wanted to show how the annual flow of national wealth could be seen to grow steadily. He explained this growth by emphasizing the division of labor as the source of a society's capacity to increase its productivity. This division of labor, of course, can occur only after a prior accumulation of capital, which is used to pay the additional workers and to buy tools and machines.

Here then was a "machine" for *growth*—a machine that operated with all the reliability of the Newtonian system with which Smith was quite familiar. Unlike the Newtonian system, however, Smith's growth machine did not depend for its operation on the laws of nature alone. Human nature drove it, and human nature was a complex rather than a simple force. Thus, the wealth of nations would grow only if individuals, represented by their governments, would refrain from inhibiting this growth by caving into demands for special privilege. Such interference would prevent the competitive system from exerting its beneficial effect.

Of course, Smith's idea of an economic "machine" based on the aggregate of individuals' self-interest was not new. It had already been introduced in 1705 by Bernard Mandeville in *The Fable of The Bees: Or Private Vices, Public Benefits*. But there were differences between the two theories. Both Smith and Mandeville believed that the sum of self-interested actions by individuals would contribute to the public good. What set Mandeville apart from Smith was his account of what ultimately drove those actions, and hence also the public good. Smith believed in a type of virtuous self-interest that results in invisible cooperation. Mandeville, on the other hand, believed that vicious greed would lead to invisible cooperation but only if properly channeled.

In Smith's secular thought, we catch glimpses of a vision of an ultimately declining rate of profit. Smith explicitly mentions the prospect that when the system eventually accumulates its "full complement of riches"—all the pin factories, so to speak, whose output could be absorbed—economic decline would then begin, culminating in an impoverished stagnation.

For Mueller, Smith's theory suffers from its secularity, or rather, from its pantheism. The self-correcting mechanism driven by its Newtonian forces had misplaced the most important virtue—charity. Smith's underlying notion of human nature assumed egoistic inclinations but neglected altruism. As such, Mueller argues, it suffered from a deep lack of understanding of how the market actually functions. Mueller instead proposes a divine element—a divine economy—and he believes that that can only be achieved by bringing charity back into the picture. He argues that buying and selling is not the only sort of exchange that constitutes an economy and that gift giving must be considered as well.[2]

In this chapter, I side with Mueller's demand for a divine economy, but disagree with the weight and importance that he assigns to gifts. My main purpose is to propose that we replace the idea of charity with generosity. Although gifts play an important role in the social sphere, they play a much smaller role in the market. In a sense, the role that they do play in the market is non-"altruistic"—as the exchangeable element of gift. Gift giving as a non-egoistic act lies beyond the market. Generosity, on the other hand, is by nature an economic act within the sphere of the market. The way it functions is not by giving money but through providing a neighbor with the opportunity to enter into the market himself.

In Mueller's survey of the history of economic thought, he emphasizes the role of use in Aquinas's theory of property and attacks Smith for disregarding distributive justice. In other words, while Mueller accepts the idea that the justification of property rights is in order to utilize the property; accumulating wealth for its own sake is, however, considered a misuse. I have already offered an analysis of the role of liberty in the Jewish idea of ownership and explained why it is liberty rather than use that generates freedom. I would like to show that from the notion of liberty arises an idea of exchange that, while permitting some measure of egoism, includes altruism as well. This altruistic element implies several values, among them trust and generosity. Thus, the market creates a space that enables free people to function as independent agents, living their lives and helping each other in the process. The two elements just mentioned—trust and generosity—are elements that function inside the market and that utilize and enhance market forces. Investment drives the market, but it is unthinkable where there is no trust and, to a certain extent, also generosity.

There is another important difference between charity and generosity. When performing charity, the focus is on the giver. In generosity, the focus is on the needy. I am thinking of the common practice whereby an older, well-to-do businessman helps a younger businessman by giving him leads or even capital. This sort of generosity is not identical with charity. It bears more similarity to a father helping his son. A community of individuals imbued with the spirit of generosity is a community with a shared moral ethos. What they have in common is not only a kinship sense of interrelation but a set of common values.

A community of generosity is also prosperous. Many times the young man who was helped climbs up the ladder of success, and ends up later helping the person who helped him. Thus, when an older person helps a young man, his act is similar to planting a tree insofar as even if the old man himself does not benefit, his children will. It is upon such acts of generosity that a healthy and prosperous society is based.

EGOISM AND ALTRUISM

Like Christianity, Judaism emphasizes charity and generosity. The biblical saying "You must love your neighbor as [you love] yourself" (Lev. 19:18) is the ultimate expression of the responsibility that one bears toward his fellow man. There is nevertheless a danger of misunderstanding this love as a negation of the self in favor of the neighbor. Jewish commentators have thus emphasized the words *as yourself* to make the point that the love toward one's neighbor should not exceed the love that one bears for oneself. Are these commentators in effect praising the relationship between two egoists?

For a careful analysis of the Jewish perception of the ethical relationship between neighbors, we ought to explore the two biblical commandments expressed in the phrases: "Love your neighbor" and "let your brother live alongside you" (Lev. 25:36). The two phrases are interpreted in a similar fashion. In both cases, traditional Jewish commentary focuses on the mutuality of the relationship—love your neighbor *as yourself*; your brother may live *with you*. There is always a "you" present against which to compare your love for your neighbor. That is why it was decided that concern for the neighbor's livelihood should not come to the detriment of one's own. Discussing the phrase, "You must love your neighbor as [you love] yourself," Nahmanides explains that this demand is hyperbole. It is impossible for a person to love his neighbor to the same degree he loves himself.[3] Nahmanides's statement makes sense because the Talmud understands the equation between the neighbor and self as a point of reference: "What is hateful to you, do not do to your neighbor":

> On another occasion it happened that a certain heathen came before Shammai and said to him, "Make me a proselyte, on condition that you teach me the whole Torah while I stand on one foot." Thereupon he repulsed him with the builder's cubit which was in his hand. When he went before Hillel, he said to him, "What is hateful to you, do not to your neighbor: that is the whole Torah, while the rest is the commentary thereof; go and learn it."[4]

The comparison between neighbor and self is understood from the word *Kamocha*—"as [you love] yourself," an idea that is also present elsewhere in the Torah. As mentioned, we also see the application of this idea in interpreting the phrase "let your brother live alongside you." In the Talmudic discussion, the son of Patura claims that one should live and die with his neighbor, while R. Akiva deduces from the phrase that one's own life is an ultimate point of reference that should not be exceeded:

> Now how does R. Johanan interpret, "let your brother live alongside you"?— He utilizes it for that which was taught: If two are traveling on a journey [far from civilization], and one has a pitcher of water, if both drink, they will [both] die, but if one only drinks, he can reach civilization,— The Son of Patura taught: It is better that both should drink and die, rather than that one should behold his companion's death. Until R. Akiba came and taught: "that thy brother may live with thee:" thy life takes precedence over his life.[5]

As we can see, all consideration for one's neighbor finds its limit at the point where it endangers one's own life.

The repetition of this idea in these two phrases, in the first with the word *Kamocha*—"as [you love] yourself," and in the other with the word *Imach*—"alongside you," strengthens the idea that for the Torah, at least according to the majority opinion of the Sages, ethical obligations toward the neighbor are qualified by the precedence of self.[6]

One must note that consideration of one's own needs does not entail egoism of any sort. It is not an *ethical egoism* that Jewish law professes. Rather it is an *altruism qualified by interest-self*. The assumption is that the needs of self should not be ignored, because if they are ignored undesired consequences may follow. Jewish law does not advocate self-interest. Indeed, the case is more nearly the opposite. A person who cares only for his self-interest is compared to an idol-worshiper.[7] Neither does Jewish law believe in a pure or absolute form of altruism. A measure of self-interest is necessary to maintain a healthy altruism.

THE MARKET—IS THERE A PLACE FOR GIVING?

As mentioned, Adam Smith's theory is best described as an analysis of the market as a self-correcting mechanism where many self-interested forces compete against each other and at the same time drive the machine forward. In this machine, there is no room for altruism. Charity, which is an act of altruism, is considered an act beyond the bounds of the market. Of course, some will claim that charity, with its beneficial effects on the happiness of givers and receivers, enhances prosperity as well, but this is not a direct influence. In fact, according to this analysis, it is the self-interest and not the altruism of the people involved with charity—both the giving and receiving parties—that helps create prosperity.

Generosity, by contrast, is an act of altruism that is *internal* to the market. It is an act that enhances prosperity in a very direct way. When people care about others, they actually care about their community. When they help others in the business world, or extend their hand to a person who wants to succeed, they do their part to help the whole community. The Talmud expresses great admiration for this type of ethical behavior:

> One day he was journeying on the road and he saw a man planting a carob tree; he asked him, How long does it take [for this tree] to bear fruit? The man replied: Seventy years. He then further asked him: Are you certain that you will live another seventy years? The man replied: I found [ready grown] carob trees in the world; as my forefathers planted these for me so I too plant these for my children.[8]

There is another story attributed to an old man who met Emperor Hadrian. Here the Sages deliberately associate generosity with political virtue. Political virtue in turn is understood as a responsibility enjoined by God:

"When ye shall come into the land, ye shall plant" (Lev. 19:23). Hadrian, (his bones be ground to dust!), once passed along the paths leading to Tiberias and saw an old man standing and digging trenches to plant shoots of fig-trees. Said he to him: "Greybeard, greybeard! If you had got up early to do the work, you would not have had to work late!" He answered him: "I have worked early and am working late, and let the Lord of Heaven do as it pleases Him." Said he to him: "By your life, old man! How old are you this day?" "Hundred years old," he answered. He said to him: "So you are a hundred years old, and yet are standing and digging trenches to plant shoots of fig-trees! Do you ever hope to eat of them?" He replied: "If I am worthy I shall eat, and if not, then so will I work for my children." He said to him: "On your life! If you are privileged to eat of them, let me know." In the course of time the trees produced figs. Said he: "Now it is time to let the king know." What did he do? He filled a basket with figs and went and stood at the gate of the palace. He was asked: "What is your business here?" He answered: "I want to come before the king." When he came in the latter asked him: "What is your business?" He answered him: "I am the old man whom you passed by as I was digging trenches to plant shoots of fig-trees, and you said to me: 'If you are privileged to eat of them let me know.' So, I have been so privileged and have eaten of them, and these figs are some of the fruit." Thereupon Hadrian exclaimed: "I command that a chair of gold be set down and that he sit on it." He further said: "I command that you empty this basket of his and fill it with denarii." His servants said to him: "Will you show all this honor to that old Jew?" He answered them: "His Creator honors him, and shall not I honor him too?"[9]

Hadrian, despite bearing the odious title of destroyer of the Temple, is introduced here as Roman emperor for his consummate appreciation of political virtue. There is no doubt that his role in the story is to emphasize the political aspect of the old man's act.

For an old man to plant trees is certainly not an act of self-interest. It serves the interest of the many. A community can prosper only if its members share virtues as a community and care for each other. They can reach prosperity only if they hope for shared success and are willing to help each other to achieve it. Competition that is based on self-interest may indeed lead to prosperity, but this prosperity can only be temporary. At the end of the day, if self-interest is not balanced by generosity, competition will numb market actors and invite disintegration and stagnation. Competition that is driven by egoistic motivation introduces vices into the market; not just wishes for prosperity. Competing agents may neutralize each other instead of getting ahead.

GENEROSITY, INTEREST, AND INVESTMENT

Investment is among the strongest motive forces of the market. However, investment is only possible if the two elements that I mentioned earlier exist—trust and generosity. There must be trust that the investment will eventually yield profit, as well as the generosity to give and not to be envious of the neighbor's success. As we will see, investment became an important devise in the Jewish economic tradition despite both legal impediments and the fear that allowing it would create a slippery slope to usury.

At first glance, investment does not seem to be encouraged by Jewish law. As is well known, the Torah encourages giving loans but is not in favor of taking interest:

> If your kinsman, being in straits, comes under your authority, and you hold him as though a resident alien, let him live by your side. Do not exact from him advance or accrued interest, but you fear your God. Let him live by your side as your kinsman.[10]

> If you lend money to My people, to the poor among you, do not act toward them as a creditor; exact no interest from them. If you take your neighbor's garment to pledge, you must return it to him before the sun sets; it is his only clothing, the sole covering for his skin. In what shall he sleep? Therefore, if he cries out to Me, I will pay heed, for I am compassionate.[11]

Lending money to the needy is a moral obligation not so different in character from providing charity. It is an obligation that should be performed from altruistic motives free of self-interest. Even reasonable rates of interest are forbidden, and it is not permitted to take pledges when the lender is slow returning the loan. Both the Talmud and the Hebrew Bible are strictly opposed and highly critical of all forms of usury and forbid the charging of interest. As a matter of fact, Jewish law was unique in antiquity in this regard. Other cultures and legal systems drew a distinction between interest and usury.[12]

Regardless of the severity of the prohibition against taking interest, history teaches us that Jews learned to evade this law, and were among the leading bankers of Europe in the Middle Ages. In the twelfth century, we find indeed an apology for this vocation, which implies that it did not yet enjoy high esteem.[13] Later on, however, a *responsum* from a prominent Rabbi (Israel Iserline, Vienna 1390–1460) ruled that money lent in the form of investment, where the lender becomes a partner of the business in which the money is invested, is not considered a loan but rather profit made from mutual property.[14] He based this decision on a Talmudic ruling regarding investment that appeals to the legal category *iska*, or an investment by a silent partner who wants to share some percentage of profit made in a profitable business:

The Nehardenas said: An 'iska is a semi loan and a semi trust, the Rabbis having made an enactment which is satisfactory to both the debtor and the creditor. Now that we say that it is a semi loan and a semi trust, if he [the trader] wishes to drink beer therewith [i.e., for the loan part] he can do so. Raba said: [No.] It is therefore called 'iska [business] because he can say to him, "I gave it to you for trading, not for drinking beer." R. Idi b. Abin said: And if he [the trader] dies, it ranks as movable property in the hands of his children. Raba said: It is therefore called 'iska, that if he dies, it shall not rank as movable property in the hands of his heirs.[15]

R. Iseline apologized for drawing attention to the *iska* contract. He feared that overuse of this legal expedient could generate a slippery slope toward legalized usury. He worried that people would take interest from ordinary loans without observing the distinction between loans and investments, as was intended in the case of an *iska*. In the end, he justified the *iska* by arguing that one should not prevent the opportunities enabled by profit sharing contracts between business partners.

The legal provision that R. Iserline established for a very specific sort of investment was indeed later applied to ordinary loans as well. R. Shaul Nathanson of Galicia ruled that any loan that is established with a written contract is an *iska*, and that if its purpose is to garner a livelihood, it has the legal status of an investment.[16]

Some Talmudic scholars criticize the decline of the prohibition on interest taking. Permitting the use of modern banking by applying the *iska* contract ruling seems to them a violation of Jewish law because it does not follow the moral principle or spirit of the biblical law. Defining all types of loans as investments, they argue, completely annuls the idea of charity expressed in the Torah. The Torah enjoins aiding needy people not only with gifts but also with loans, to the end of preserving their dignity. Agreeing with this criticism in principle, and urging Jewish communities to create charity funds that offer loans to the needy in addition to distributing alms, R. Baruch Epstein (Belarus 1860–1942) nevertheless justified the popularity of the *iska* expedient. According to him, a strict prohibition on charging interest would be anachronistic. The Torah law suits a rural society in which loans are a very important tool for reciprocal aid. Agriculture is by nature a speculative venture. One never knows if the labor invested in the crop will yield a good return. As R. Epstein put it, farmers work not for money but the harvest. Providing interest-free loans was just a way to regain the produce that had been lost in a bad year. Savings were never invested. Mainly they served as insurance for lean years. In addition to this explanation, we should note that in antiquity, crop failure often led to slavery. A perfectly successful farmer could lose all that he had in one bad year, and in such a case would have to sell himself into slavery. The Torah's insistence on providing loans in fact aims at the prevention of slavery.

In the Middle Ages, the market underwent many transformations and became more money and capital based. To offer a loan to a neighbor was no longer merely to offer him a superfluous item set aside for bad days. It was now to hand over the main tool—the capital—by which one earned one's livelihood. In other words, in a market society, a loan is not an act of charity but rather a method of planning and of profiting from the future. It is usually an investment.[17] That is why, according to R. Epstein, what the Rabbis did by slowly permitting the circumvention of the law forbidding interest reflected a deep understanding of changes in market conditions.

INVESTMENT AS A FORM OF GENEROSITY

Investment may indeed be considered an expression of generosity. Charity in our sense is not just adherence to a formal law but the expression of a charitable heart. Thus, it is said by Maimonides that the best way to give charity is to help the needy become independent financially, not only by giving a donation but by giving him a loan or finding him a source of income:

> There are eight levels of virtue in charity; one is greater than the other. The highest value belongs to the one who supports the Israelite who is going under, and gives him a gift or a loan, or makes a partnership with him or finds him a vocation, in order to help him so that he will not become needy.[18]

Helping a person avoid poverty is much greater than helping a person who is already poor. Investing in a person in order to help him make a living is the greatest charity. Maimonides' ruling was upheld in later writings as well, for example by R. Moshe from Coucy (1200–)[19] and in the Shulchan Aruch.[20] Similar ideas are quoted later in the writings of R. Yechiel Michael Epstein[21] who quotes a passage from the Talmud in support of Maimonides: "R. Abba also said in the name of R. Simeon b. Lakish: He who lends [money] is greater than he who performs charity; and he who forms a partnership is greater than all."[22]

R. Epstein explains that helping a person with an investment rather than giving him charity is helping him while maintaining his honor. The fact that the investor benefits as well does not diminish his merit; he helps the needy without causing shame and embarrassment.[23]

There is another reason for the preference for investment over charity. When one gives charity, he might be focused on himself rather than on the poor—he might, for example, be using the needy person as an object to perform a good deed in his own honor. This is not the case with an investor. When he makes an investment, he focuses on getting the needy person back on track, wishing for him to restore his honor and self-sufficiency.

Indeed, helping the needy become financially independent is the most valuable type of charity. Here I am not primarily interested in grading the merit of the donor. I raise the point in order to draw out the legal implications of this fact in Jewish law. When a community collected money for charity, they debated the question of who should receive the aid. Should the money go to a person who is already impoverished, or to a person who is not yet impoverished but stands in imminent danger of falling under? The Rabbinic injunction is to help the latter first. This is evident in a decision written by R. Moshe Sofer (Frankfurt and Frewsburg 1762–1839):

> Any time that [the needy person] doesn't request money from strangers and receives his provisions modestly from his relatives and maintains an appearance of prosperity, such a person falls under the definition of the rule "and you should hold him," that his relatives are obligated to support him that he will not fall under as Rashi said in his commentary on Leviticus. There is an obligation to give him priority over other people of need, because that [help] will help him to re-gain his self-sufficiency henceforth. But if one helps an ordinary needy, the help is temporary.[24]

Granting priority to a person who is struggling to maintain his self-sufficiency is of course based on personal considerations, that is, helping the one who is more ashamed first. There is a communal value as well, as is evident in the point alluded to by R. Moshe Sofer regarding the permanent versus the temporary. As I will show, a concern for communal virtues is deeply rooted in the Sages' thought.

THE POLITICAL ASPECT

Thus far we have discussed some of the virtues of investment insofar as the individual is concerned. Focusing on the good of the needy person, we can see how investment truly helps him not only in restoring his life at present but also for the future. Investment has another virtue: to secure the good of the community.[25] Communal prosperity is usually the result of the efforts of many people. Moreover, when someone helps his neighbor and gives him a loan as an investment, he has a larger picture in mind. He not only thinks about the present and the future but also about the good that will accrue to the market as a whole. He cannot be aware of all the consequences that will be engendered by his act. But he does know that restoring the needy person to a state where he might become a prosperous businessman will put him in the position to help others. Such an act is very similar to the planting of a tree mentioned earlier in this chapter. When the old man planted the tree, he thought about future generations, not about himself.

Concern for the communal good is considered a very important virtue generally in Jewish thought and law. Talmudic Sages spoke very highly of communal values, not dissimilarly to the way these virtues were praised in Hellenistic thought. "*Tikun Olam*" building the world, is a notion deeply linked to Judaism's highest theological values.[26] It is considered an example of *imitatio dei*, an imitation of the ways of God. The Sages were very much aware that concern for political virtues as *imitatio dei* was a sentiment they shared with the Romans. That is why in the story of the old man and Hadrian quoted earlier, it is Hadrian, the Roman emperor, who expresses appreciation for the act of planting a tree for generations to come. It is this type of political virtue that generates political power from bottom up. Note, however, that the Agadic story opened with the biblical verse: "When ye shall come into the land, ye shall plant" (Lev. 19:23). Planting a tree is an obligation that is connected to entering the land. It also recalls the way God as the creator of the world planted

trees and thus enjoins *imitatio dei*. Hadrian said to his people: "His Creator honors him, and shall not I honor him too?"[27] With this phrase, an agreement is expressed between God and the emperor regarding the virtue of planting trees, that is, of the political virtue of thinking about the future and the good of the whole people. This holds even in those instances when the particular good will not necessarily benefit the person who makes the effort and plants the tree.

Yet, concern for the political good, as important as it is, can sometimes become counterproductive. Although concern about the next generation and the future is valued highly, there is a stream of Talmudic thought that perceives preoccupation with the future as hubris. According to the source quoted below, though, human beings should concern themselves with their own duties, rather than the Lord's plans:

> R. Hamnuna said: What is the meaning of the verse, Who is as the wise man? And who knoweth the interpretation [pesher] of a thing? Who is like the Holy One, blessed be He, who knew how to effect a reconciliation [pesharah] between two righteous men, Hezekiah and Isaiah? Hezekiah said: Let Isaiah come to me, for so we find that Elijah went to Ahab, as it says, And Elijah went to show himself unto Ahab. Isaiah said: Let Hezekiah come to me, for so we find that Jehoram son of Ahab went to Elisha. What did the Holy One, blessed be He, do? He brought sufferings upon Hezekiah and then said to Isaiah, Go visit the sick. For so it says, In those days was Hezekiah sick unto death. And Isaiah the prophet, son of Amoz, came to him and said unto him, Thus saith the Lord, Set thy house in order, for thou shalt die and not live etc. What is the meaning of "thou shalt die and not live"? Thou shalt die in this world and not live in the world to come. He (Hezekiah) said to him: Why so bad? He replied: Because you did not try to have children. He (Isaiah) said: The reason was because I saw by the Holy Spirit that the children issuing from me would not be virtuous. He said to him: What have you to do with the secrets of the All-Merciful? You should have done what you were commanded, and let the Holy One, blessed be He, do that which pleases Him. He said to him: Then give me now your daughter; perhaps through your merit and mine combined virtuous children will issue from me. He replied: The doom has already been decreed. Said the other (Hezekiah): Son of Amoz (Isaiah), finish your prophecy and go. This tradition I have from the house of my ancestor: Even if a sharp sword rests upon a man's neck he should not desist from prayer.[28]

Here the Talmud makes it clear that a person should not meddle with God's plans. As Isaiah expresses it: "What have you to do with the secrets of the All-Merciful? You should have done what you were commanded, and let the Holy One, blessed be He, do that which pleases Him."

Many infer from this that a person should avoid concerning himself with politics,[29] a stance very much opposed to the cultivation of political virtue. Is this really what the text means to say? If not, what is the meaning of these statements? Considering the text about the old man and Hadrian alongside the text about

Hezekiah and Isaiah will help us shed light on this question. It seems to me that political virtues are so emphatically appreciated by a wide variety of Talmudic sources that we should not doubt the value the Talmud places in them. What was wrong with Hezekiah was not that he thought about the future good. Rather he exceeded his bounds as a human being when he made predications that were no longer based on rational calculations. Nonrational knowledge of the future belongs to God. Man has to stick to the rational and abide by it. In doing so, he also has to demonstrate concern not only for himself but for the larger community as well. Yet again, no one should sacrifice his personal needs for the sake of the communal. "If a man offered all his wealth for love, He would be laughed to scorn."[30] For our purposes, offering wealth for love of the many is no better than doing so for the love of an individual.

How then is the correct balance to be found between concern for the many and a struggling individual's concern for himself? In what proportion should we divide our efforts between the private and public spheres? I have already discussed the distinction introduced by Talmudic sources between helping needy relatives and helping the poor of the city or the greater community. In that case, the distinction was introduced by the members of the community itself. It is a quantitative solution rather than a qualitative one. What is important is that the individual show concern for the political in addition to his concern for his private good, and yet do so without engaging in self-abnegation.

CONCLUSION: ORGANIZED ORDER AND SPONTANEOUS ORDER

Concern for the common good, the political good, is not based on a specific quantitative need but a general one. When the polity develops in a certain direction, it is important that all the individuals comprising that community do their part. If the individuals resist the collective good and direct their energies solely to their own benefit, no collective good will ever be achieved, or at the very least will be severely retarded. A community is a body that exists on the basis of a common idea or a common ethos. Every part of the whole has to participate in the common idea or ethos for it to succeed. The importance and significance of generosity is that it is a virtue that can serve as a vector guiding our striving toward a common good and a common prosperity.

A person who helps his neighbor and makes an investment in him does not always know if his investment will bear fruit. He does so because he has some vague idea of the future development of the market, which remains a spontaneous order. Only intuition can help him judge in advance how fruitful the investment will be. The next chapter turns to consider the spontaneity of the market and the importance of spontaneous order.

NOTES

1. John D. Mueller, *Redeeming Economics, Rediscovering the Missing Element*, Wilmington (ISI Books: 2010), 17–26.

2. Mueller is not alone in his search for value. Amartya Sen shares with him a similar sentiment. See Amartya Sen, *On Ethics and Economics* (Oxford: Blackwell, 1988), 41–50, 78–89.

3. R. Moshe B. Nahman—Nahmanides, *Commentary to the Torah*, Leviticus 19:18.

4. *BT*, Shabbat, 31a.

5. *BT*, Babba Mezia, 62b.

6. Rabies in the Middle Ages combined these two phrases in order to achieve such a deduction. See R. Moshe B. Nachman, ibid.

7. *BT*, Sota 5a.

8. *BT*, Taanith 23a.

9. Midrash Rabbah, *Leviticus 25* (London: Soncino Press, 1939).

10. Leviticus 25:35–36.

11. Exodus 22:24–26.

12. R. Maloney "Usury and Restrictions on Interest Taking in the Near East" *CBQ* 36 (1974): 1.

13. R. Yakov Tam, Tos. Baba Mezia, 70b, D'H Tashich: "[S]ince we have to pay [high] taxes, and all that we gain is for our mere livelihood. And more else, that we live among the nations, and we can't make our living if we'll not have business connections with them. Therefore we shouldn't limit interest, that one might learn bad behavior from them, more than any other business interaction."

14. R. Israel Iserline, Terumat HaDeshen, 302.

15. *BT*, Baba Mezia 104b. For the Halakhah decision see R. Yosef Karo, Shulchan Aruch, Yore Dea, 177.

16. R. Saul Nathanson, Shoel UMeshiv 1st. ed. 3 vol. si. 160.

17. R. Baruch Epstein, *Torah Temima*, Leviticus, chap. 25, n. 192.

18. Maimonides, *Mishne Torah*, Matnot Aniyim 10:7.

19. R. Moshe Coucy, Sefer Mitzvot Gadol, *Positive Commandments*, 162.

20. R. Yosef Karo, *Shulchan Aruch*, Yore De'a 249:6.

21. R. Yechiel Michael Epstein, *Aroch HaShilchan*, 249:14.

22. *BT*, Shabbat 63a.

23. Rashi, ibid; R. *Yosef Karo*, Bet Yosef, Yore De'a, 249.

24. R. Moshe Sofer, Shut Hatam Sofer, vol. B Yore De'a, 239, R. Shmuel Vozner, Shut Shevet HaLevi, vol. 5, 138.

25. On the obligation to help as a preventative action and its connection to a communal responsibility see Pinchas HaLevi Horwitz, Panim Yafot, *Leviticus 25*.

26. On Tikun Olam see Mishna Gitin 4:3; *BT*, Gitin 33b, Gitin 45a.

27. Midrash Rabbah, *Leviticus 25*.

28. *BT*, Berachot 10b.

29. See for instance R. Shmuel Segal, Nahalat Shiv'a, new response, 1.

30. Song of Songs 8:7.

5

COMPETITION

A cursory reading of Talmudic sources does not immediately reveal a high opinion of the free market. Talmudic Sages permitted the limitation of competition in the market, encouraged price regulation of basic goods, and appear to have viewed the market itself as a closed entity. The general impression produced by this reading is of Talmudic support for a highly regulated market. On the other hand, the Talmud presents other views that by no means dovetail with classical notions of a controlled market.[1] Here the Talmud encourages individuality in economic activity. Indeed, in matters where a higher value is at stake (such as education), it encourages competition.

These seeming exceptions to the apparent support for market control are not exceptions to the rule. They are based on far deeper underlying theological ideas. This chapter considers both sides of the equation. We examine the sources that seem to be in favor of a controlled market and those that support economic freedom. At the same time, we argue that the sources favoring a controlled market should be understood within the historical context in which they appear. Sources that favor freedom, by contrast, are shown to reflect a theory.

LIMITING COMPETITION

Talmudic law limits free competition in two ways. The first consists in direct limitations on competition; the second is price control. It is important to note at the outset that the cases in which competition is limited rest on an appeal to property rights.

There are relatively few Talmudic allusions to issues of economic competition *per se*. Some of these raise the question of the permissible limits of the use of advertizing. The Mishnah describes a dispute among the Sages regarding situations in which advertisement is permitted, in this case in the form of distributing presents to children. By doing so, the shopkeeper hopes that when the parents send these same children to buy goods for the household, they will choose him and buy his merchandise:

> R. Judah says that a shopkeeper must not distribute parched corn or nuts to children, because he accustoms them thereby to come [and buy] at his place; but the Sages allow it! And he must not lower the price, but the Sages say, He is to be remembered for good. (Misnah, Baba Mezia 4:12)[2]

The law was determined according to the opinion of the Sages. The Talmud elaborates on their opinion: "The Rabbis allowed the shopkeeper to do this, for he can say to his rival, 'Just as I make presents of nuts so you can make presents of almonds.'"[3]

Nevertheless, R. Judah is not the only Sage to oppose advertising. Abba Saul holds that even improving the appearance of the merchandise ought to be considered deception: "[A shopkeeper] must not sift pounded beans according to the view of Abba Saul; but the Sages permit it, nevertheless they admit that he may not sift them only from the top of the bin since this is intended only to mislead the eye [of the buyer]."[4]

Of course, this dispute is different from the previous one. Here the worry is that improving the appearance of the merchandise will lead to deception, though here again the law was determined according to the opinion of the Sages.[5] As we will see, such limitations to the free market are not intended to respond to a threat from above. Rather, they are motivated by the fear of injustice. The basic concern is that competition will lead to deception. When R. Judah or R. Abba Saul forbid competition, they are not disagreeing with the Sages regarding the economic efficiency of this or that system. Instead, they are responding to a concern of injustice.

The mere fact of R. Judah and R. Abba Saul's opinions that advertisement may be forbidden is likely to immediately raise modern eyebrows. Joseph Menirav claims that in places where the mobility of merchandise was limited (as was the case in Palestine of the second and third centuries), competition could indeed lead to the inability of a shopkeeper to sell his products. Because the shopkeeper was prevented from selling his merchandise in external markets, he would therefore have had to close his shop.[6]

Reading Menirav's claim in context of this source alone might create the impression that it is merely apologetic. If we place it within the context of a plurality of sources, however, it ought to correctly inform our perspective on the Talmudic idea of competition. Advertizing in the markets of the Hellenistic world was much more common than is usually appreciated; Jewish environments were no different in this regard. The activity of sales promotion was in fact no less popular in antiquity than today (although naturally the means were different). It is true that our knowledge of the methods of sales promotion and of augmenting the closing ratio at this period in history is not vast; the evidence, however, suffices for a general picture. We find remains of wall murals in Pompey that advertised politicians, writings on the walls advertising gladiator competitions and public baths, as well as many private advertisements. Among these there are hosting services, wine price lists on the walls of a winery, as well as names of businesses. Of course, remains of this sort did not survive in Palestine, but written sources exist confirming similar activity. In the Palestinian Talmud, for instance, we find the following quote: At the time of R. Jochanan they allowed drawing on walls, and they did not protest against it.[7]

While drawing on walls was no doubt done for artistic purposes, it was also used for advertisement. As Menirav claims, advertising was highly developed and he proves that besides visual advertisements there were vocal ones as well.[8] In two cases, Talmudic sources describe merchants shouting and yelling for customers, as is so common in Levantine markets to this day.[9] In this context, R. Judah and R. Abba Saul's opinion that advertisement is forbidden appears incongruous. When the Sages allow advertisement, they allow an established custom and are thus within the cultural mainstream.

COMMUNAL LIMITS OF COMPETITION

Another category of limitations on competition is communally based. In some cases, the Talmud allows neighbors, residents of the same city, or even guild members to prevent an outsider from doing business. An example of the first is found in laws of damages:

> [If one desires to establish] a shop within a courtyard, another may protest against him and say to him, "I am unable to sleep on the account of the noise of those coming in and because of the noise of those going out. But one who makes utensils [in his house] and goes forth and sells them in the market, none may protest against him and say to him, 'I cannot sleep on the account of noise from the hammer,' or '… because of the noise of the (hand) mill,' or, '… by reason of the noise from the children.'"[10]

The claim against establishing a shop in a courtyard is apparently due to the damage that arises from noise. The Mishna is not concerned here with two businesses competing against each other; it is responding to residents' complaints against a noisy business in a residential area. This Mishna was nevertheless the occasion for a much more developed discussion in the Talmud. In this discussion, the dispute is no longer between a shopkeeper and a resident who desires peaceful nights. Instead, it is between two businesses in competition. Here a new claim comes to the fore: "You are interfering with my livelihood":

> R. Huna said: If a resident of an alley sets up a hand-mill and another resident
> of the alley wants to set up one next to him, the first has the right to stop
> him, because he can say to him, "You are interfering with my livelihood."
> May we say that this view is supported by the following: "Fishing nets
> must be kept away from [the hiding-place of] a fish [which has been spotted
> by another fisherman] the full length of the fish's swim." And how much
> is this? Rabbah son of R. Huna says: A parasang?—Fishes are different,
> because they look about [for food].[11]

This new claim of "You are interfering with my livelihood" is revealing insofar
as it reflects a number of assumptions. It presumes that there exists a fixed amount
of income that one can make from his profession, and that the addition of competing
businesses necessarily reduces this income. Furthermore, as Menirav argued, this
rule applies only in places where the mobility of merchandise is limited. In such
situations, competition could indeed lead to the inability of one of the shopkeepers
to sell his products. Immobility could prevent him from selling his merchandise
in external markets, and he would therefore be forced to close his business.[12] In
those cases were mobility exists, as with fishermen whose source of income is
not confined to one area, the claim of "You are interfering with my livelihood" is
invalid. The Talmud only reluctantly accepts the claim of interference with livelihood. When competition is fair, it is permitted. Competition is only limited in cases
where livelihood cannot be made in a specific area:

> Said Rabina to Raba: May we say that R. Huna adopts the same principle
> as R. Judah? For we have learnt: R. Judah says that a shopkeeper should
> not give presents of parched corn and nuts to children, because he thus
> entices them to come back to him. The Sages, however, allow this!—You
> may even say that he is in agreement with the Rabbis also. For the ground
> on which the Rabbis allowed the shopkeeper to do this was because he can
> say to his rival, Just as I make presents of nuts so you can make presents
> of almonds; but in this case they would agree that the first man can say to
> the other. "You are interfering with my livelihood."[13]

Even the claim of interference with livelihood is challenged in the Talmud on
the basis of property rights. Prevention of competition is seen as an infringement
of liberty itself:

> An objection was raised [against Rab Huna's ruling from the following:] "A
> man may open a shop next to another man's shop or a bath next to another
> man's bath, and the latter cannot object. Because he can say to him, I do
> what I like in my property and you do what you like in yours?"—On this
> point there is a difference of opinion among Tannaim, as appears from the
> following Baraitha: "The residents of an alley can prevent one another from
> bringing in a tailor or a tanner or a teacher or any other craftsman, but one
> cannot prevent another [from setting up in opposition]." Rabban Simeon
> b. Gamaliel, however, says that one may prevent another.[14]

Here the Talmud presents a dispute among the early Sages—the Tannaim. Claims for interference with livelihood can never be accepted, according to some Sages if the disputants are both residences of the same city. Nevertheless, one can claim interference against a competitor from a different city. Rabban Simeon b. Gamaliel, however, disagrees and contends that everyone has a right to claim for interference with livelihood, even against a neighbor. The law in the Talmud was decided in favor of the Sages and against Rabban Simeon b. Gamaliel, as we gather from R. Huna the son of R. Joshua in the text below:

> R. Huna the son of R. Joshua said: It is quite clear to me that the resident of one town can prevent the resident of another town [from setting up in opposition in his town] not, however, if he pays taxes to that town—and that the resident of an alley cannot prevent another resident of the same alley [from setting up in opposition in his alley].[15]

The law as formulated allows a claim for interference with livelihood against strangers but not against people from the same city. The meaning of the ruling is that a claim for interference with livelihood does not stand independently without the support of property rights. When such a claim is applied against a person who has similar rights—the claim falls. It stands only against a person who has no rights in the given situation. In other words, it is not really the claim for interference with livelihood that enables a person to protect himself from competition but the fact that he has rights to his property. Thus, the reason for allowing protection against competition is primarily based on legality of rights of residence.

Therefore, we see that the reason for limiting competition is not derived from economics but rather from law. Residents have a legal right to prevent competition from strangers. The Talmudic Sages did not base their ruling on the idea that limiting competition is good for economy, but they did contend that in certain cases that some have rights of protection against competition. It appears then that the Talmud is indifferent to the question of whether competition is actually good for the economy.

Closer reading of the Talmudic Sages, however, indicates that they did indeed believe that competition is good for the economy, while simultaneously holding that certain property rights may be a source of immunity from certain forms of competition regardless of the economic benefits. This attitude is not exclusively Talmudic. Jewish communities in medieval Europe applied a judicial rule called *Hezkat Yishuv* (right of residency) to prevent new Jewish settlers in the medieval cities. They applied the right *Herem Yishuv* against immigrants.[16] New settlers meant new competitors for the local wealth, which the established residents were unwilling to share. *Hezkat Yishuv* was accepted by many Rabbinic authorities. It also, however, drew fierce opposition from others, including some of the greatest Sages. Rabenu Asher (Germany and Toledo, 1250–1327) for instance, described such measures as a disgrace:

It is very clear that every man is permitted to leave his town and move to another town, and the burgers can't prevent him from living among them while claiming that he disturbs their livelihood, because the land is not given to them only. All (the Jewish people) belong to one governor that they all pay him tax that is imposed upon them.[17]

Herem Hayishuv or *Hezkat Hayishuv* seems to represent an anticompetition stance. Here we seem to have a medieval Jewish community attempting to protect its members' economic rights in an absolute fashion, but the picture is much more complicated than that. As Simcha Goldin illustrates, preventing people from joining the community in many instances was not based on economic grounds so much as on social grounds. According to Goldin, the social factor was decisive, and the *Herem Hayishuv* measure's purpose was to foster the social bond of a community.[18] Regardless of such qualifications, an anticompetition stance continued in the Jewish communities in Poland until the modern era.[19]

There are two cases where the Talmudic Sages permit competition irrespective of property rights. One is competition in education and the other is competition in perfume selling. "R. Joseph said: R. Huna agrees that a teacher cannot prevent [another teacher from setting up in the same alley], for the reason mentioned, That 'the jealousy of scribes increaseth wisdom.'"[20]

This old decree (attributed to Ezra the Scribe) stipulates that teachers should compete. Reading the phrase—"the jealousy of scribes increaseth wisdom"—the Sages deduced that competition in teaching is good for education. Because education is a value, an ideal, it overrides property rights. Likewise in the case of selling perfume:

> R. Nahman b. Isaac said: R. Huna the son of R. Joshuah also agrees that itinerant spice-sellers cannot prevent one another from going to any given town, because, as a Master has stated, Ezra made a rule for Israel that spice-sellers should go about from town to town so that the daughters of Israel should be able to obtain finery. This, however, only means that they are at liberty to go from house to house [in the strange town], but not to settle there. If, however, the seller is a student, he may settle also, a precedent having been set by Raba in allowing R. Josiah and R. Obadiah to settle, in spite of the rule. The reason he gave was that, as they were Rabbis, they would be disturbed in their studies [if they had to return to their own town].[21]

The selling of perfumes and cosmetics is granted value because it helps to maintain family values. Here again, matters of value override property rights.

Why, we should ask, is the Talmud not concerned about prosperity as an ideal value in the same way it is concerned about Torah learning or about family life? Is it possible that prosperity is not in itself a value for the Talmud Sages? It is easy to prove that this is not the case: "Why then is it laid down that creditors for loans are paid out of the medium quality? This is a Rabbinic enactment made in order that prospective borrowers should not find the door of their benefactors locked before them."[22] This is one case where the Sages ruled in favor of lenders to prevent a shortage of available loans. Availability of loans is of course of social value, but the reasoning "that prospective borrowers should not find the door of their benefactors locked before them," is also applied beyond cases of loans and is extended as a principle of civil law in general.[23]

The Talmudic view is thus that limits on competition do not apply where they stand in the way of increased prosperity. The claim of interference with livelihood is valid only in markets operating under conditions of immobility.

PRICE REGULATION

Just as the limited right to circumscribe competition derives from property rights, the communal right to price controls on the exchange of certain goods is derived from the same consideration. Controlling prices is neither recommended nor advised in the Talmud. It is described as a communal legal right—not as an economic virtue. There is, however, one exception. The Sages make provision for common price control of basic economic goods, as was done throughout the Roman Empire. The first source for price control is a Tanaitic source that is found in the Talmud:

> Our Rabbis taught: [...] The townspeople, however, are at liberty to use the soup kitchen like the charity fund and vice versa, and to apply them to whatever purposes they choose. The townspeople are also at liberty to fix weights and measures, prices, and wages, and to inflict penalties for the infringement of their rules.[24]

The liberty possessed by the townspeople stems from a common property that created a sort of a partnership. Price control is not enforced by a Rabbinic court but by the free will of townspeople. The Talmud merely states that the townspeople have a right to institute rules of control.

In the case of basic goods, the story is different. The Talmud teaches us that in Palestine there was a decree against making high profits in the sale of necessities:

> Our Rabbis taught: In Palestine it is not permitted to make a profit [as middleman] in things which are life's necessaries, such as, for instance, wines, oils and the various kinds of flour. It has been said about R. Eleazar b. Azariah that he used to make a profit in wine and oil. In [the case of] wine he held the same opinion as R. Judah; in [the case of] oil?—In the place of R' Eleazar b. Azariah oil was plentiful. Our Rabbis taught: It is not permitted to make a profit in eggs twice. [As to the meaning of "twice,"] Mari b. Mari said: Rab and Samuel are in dispute. One says: Two for one. And the other says: [Selling] by a dealer to a dealer.[25]

This source seems to locate price control in Palestine, though another source (earlier in the same tractate) discusses a dispute arising over this debate and implies that price control is recommended everywhere:

> Our Rabbis taught: *Thou shalt have*, teaches that market officers are appointed to [superintend] measures, but no such officers are appointed for [superintending] prices. Those of the Nasi's [President's] House appointed market officers to [superintend] both measures and prices. [Thereupon] said Samuel to Karna: Go forth and teach them [the law that] market officers are appointed to [superintend] measures, but no such officers are appointed to [superintend] prices. [But Karna] went forth [and] gave them the [following] exposition: Market officers are appointed to [superintend] both measures and prices. He said unto him: Is your name Karna? Let a horn grow out of your eye. A horn, [consequently] grew out of his eye. But whose opinion did he follow?—That voiced by Rami b. Hama in the name of R. Isaac that market officers are appointed to [superintend] both measures and prices, on account of the impostors.[26]

The law was indeed adopted. This meant that price control was enforced in Palestine and everywhere else:

> We have already explained that an honest salesman, who declares how much he profits, does not have to worry about claims of fraud, even if he declares that he sells for ten what he bought for four. But the court has to fix prices and enforce them so profit will not depend on free will of every person, but rather a sixth of the price should be fixed. A seller should not profit more than a sixth.
>
> It is forbidden to sell things which are life's necessaries as merchandise, but each farmer sells his own produce, so he can sell cheaply. In a place that oil is cheap, one may make profit from selling oil.[27]

From this source, we learn that price control is favored by the Sages. In this respect, they mirrored a common practice in the Roman Empire.

In the context, however, of the wide-ranging price regulations of the Roman Empire,[28] it is the *limitation* of control to essential items that should capture our attention, rather than the mere fact that prices are controlled. Of course, Jewish Law is not in principle opposed to regulating prices (*laissez faire* is hardly a Jewish motto!). How much does this particular regulation suggest an attempt to impose all-embracing market controls?

We should recall is that the fundamental aim of all the sources cited thus far is judicial: namely, the protection of individual rights. Neither strictly economic concerns, economic prosperity, nor freedom within or of the market are addressed in these sources. The reason is not that the Talmudic Sages were unconcerned with economic prosperity. The cause of their silence is that they did not believe that economic prosperity rested in man's hands.

THE SWORD AND ECONOMIC PROSPERITY

The Talmud is sparse when it comes to discussions about methods of creating economic prosperity. For the Talmudic Sages, the way to achieve prosperity (besides through God's help) was mainly through war. Thus the Talmudic Sages explain how King David achieved prosperity in his days:

> For so said R. Aha b. Bizna in the name of R. Simeon the Pious: a harp was hanging above David's bed. As soon as midnight arrived, a North wind came and blew upon it and it played of itself. He arose immediately and studied the Torah till the break of dawn. After the break of dawn the wise men of Israel came in to see him: Our lord, the King, Israel your people require sustenance! He said to them: Let them go out and make a living one from the other. They said to him: A handful cannot satisfy a lion, nor can a cistern be filled up with its own clods. He said to them: Then go out in troops and attack [the enemy for plunder].[29]

King David initially recommends to his people that they go out and make a living one from the other; he seems, however, to think that making a living in this way does not lead to prosperity. It only maintains life as it is. To realize prosperity, he suggests war.

An interesting parallel exists between this passage and one in Plato's *Republic*. There, Socrates paints a picture of an idyllic but rustic community. When Glaucon complains that he wants better food, better furnishings, and in general, sensory and aesthetic pleasure, Socrates argues that such "over-stepping of the boundaries of necessity" leads to violence and war.[30] Aiming for more than the necessary minimum for the arts will lead to the use of the sword. Eventually, this military life will itself set limits to the pursuit of luxury.[31]

This whole open-ended dynamic is founded on a certain concept of the market. The kind of communal self-sufficiency associated in the Greek imagination with an independent household is shown in the *Republic* to be impossible. One will always need some foreign imports. Because one can never know in advance the origin and price of these imports, the city requires built-in flexibility and service orientation. This, however, is beyond the capacities of the merely communal city; it also necessitates market exchange. The possibility of acquisition that leads to the pursuit of luxury and then to war is thus a consequence of the market economy.[32]

Plato does not discuss the details of economic exchange. As previously noted, economics as a theory did not exist before Aquinas and in its more developed form until the modern state came into being.[33] Nevertheless, discussions of the sort that Plato develops are absent in Jewish sources. What exists instead is discussion of the religious side of economics: in other words, the effects of the relationship between man and God on the economy.

GOD AND ECONOMIC PROSPERITY

Jewish faith is based on the assumption that God intervenes in the world; hence, prosperity depends on him. At the same time, Jewish faith is not fatalistic. God does not help a person who does not work hard, as the Sages put it. Only being diligent in commerce alongside prayer to God leads to wealth:

> What must a man do that he may become rich? He replied: Let him engage much in business and deal honestly. Did not many, they said to him, do so but it was of no avail to them?—Rather, let him pray for mercy from Him to whom all riches belong, for it is said, Mine is the silver, and Mine the gold. What then does he teach us?—That one without the other does not suffice.[34]

As we have seen, commerce is not enough to increase public prosperity. The Sages also believed in faith. If a person were meant to be wealthy, wealth would come to him:

> Our Rabbis taught: The house of Abtinas were expert in preparing the incense but would not teach [their art]. The Sages sent for specialists from Alexandria of Egypt, who knew how to compound incense as well as they, but did not know how to make the smoke ascend as well as they. The smoke of the former ascended [as straight] as a stick, wheres the smoke of the latter was scattered in every direction. When the sages heard thereof, they quoted: "Every one that is called My name, I have created for My glory" (Proverbs 16). As it said The Lord hath made everything for His own purpose. And [said]: The house of Abtinas may return to their [wonted] place. The Sages sent for them, but they wouldn't come. Then they doubled their hire and they came. Every day [thitherto] they would receive twelve minas, [from] that day twenty-four. The Sages said to them: What reason did you have for not teaching [your art]? They said: They knew in our father's house that this House is going to be destroyed and they said: Perhaps an unworthy man will learn [this art] and will serve an idol therewith.—and for the following reason was their memory kept in honour: Never did a bride of their house go forth perfumed and when they married a woman from elsewhere they expressly forbade her to do so lesst people say: From [the preparation of] the incense they are perfuming themselves. [They did so] to fulfill the command: "Ye shall be clear before the Lord and before Israel." … Referring to this Ben Azzai said: By your name you will be called, to your place you will be restored, and from what belongs to you will you be given. No man can touch what is prepared for his fellow and "One kingdom does not interfere with the other even to the extent of ones hair's breadth."[35]

A person gets what is prepared for him, at least so far as his private fortune is concerned. What, one might ask, about the public fortune? The Sages demand public prayer when the economy fails to function.[36] They never recommend a policy of working harder or of manipulating the market to facilitate prosperity. It seems that they considered the public economic welfare to be much more dependent on God's will than on either hard work or fate. As far as the broad public is concerned, only the hand of God can change a society's economic destiny:

> For so it happened in the days of Simeon b. Shetach. [At that time] rain fell on the eve of Wednesdays and Sabbaths so that the grains of wheat came up large as kidneys and the grains of barley like the stones of olive, and of the lentils like the golden denarii and they stored specimens of them for future generations in order to make known unto them the effects of sin, as it is said: "Your iniquities have turned away these things and your sins have withholden good from you."[37]

In a similar text, the Sages ascribe sole responsibility for a good agriculture yield to God:

> "I will grant," I, not with a help of an angel or a messenger. "Rain for your land," and not rain for other lands. As it says: "who gives rain to the face of earth, and sends water over the fields" (Job 5:10). R. Nathan says: "in season"—[rain fell] from one eve Sabbath to one eve Sabbath as it fell in the days of queen Shlemzo. Why is it so? Rabbi says: so people will not be able to question the idea of reward for observing all the commandments of the Torah. But is says instead "If you follow My laws and faithfully observe My commandments, I will grant your rains in their season, so that earth shall yield its produce and the trees of field their fruit" (Leviticus 26:3–4). "If then, you obey the commandments" (Deuteronomy 11:13) "I will grant the rain for your land in season, the early rain and the late" (ibid 11:14). How do we know that one blessing was given to Israel a blessing that includes all blessing? That is why it came to teach us "A lover of money never has his fill of money, nor a lover of wealth his fill of income." (Ecclesiastes 5:9). And it is said "thus the greatest advantage in all the land is his: he controls a field that is cultivated" (ibid 8). Here we learn that one blessing was given to Israel a blessing that includes all blessing.[38]

This Midrash is a commentary on the passage from Deuteronomy: "I will grant the rain for your land in season, the early rain and the late" (Deut. 11:14). It starts by emphasizing God's particular and exclusive attention toward the Jewish nation. It is God himself who is in charge of the rain in the land of Israel, and he takes special care over this responsibility. Rains fall during the times that everybody is at home; in this case, the Sabbath eve. The rain given to Israel is not only an agricultural blessing, but also an aid to the progress of the economy—it means silver and gold.

Commerce is not mentioned in a clear fashion here, but seems to be implied. Can we deduce from this passage that even the market is in the hands of God? With regard to the individual, diligence contributes to success when combined with prayer.

Given these considerations, it may well be that, instead of searching for concepts of the free market in the history of Jewish Law, we should try to reconstruct it anew from the world of the principles of Jewish law. Just as Novak cautions Christians about drawing too many economic deductions from the pre-capitalist world,[39] Jewish thinkers should be cautious about the economic inferences they draw from Jewish sources. Instead, we should focus on and learn from the moral principles that generated those laws. We can, for instance, deduce principles suggesting that humanity ought to be cautious about its ability to plan economies or control the market. As illustrated in this chapter, God's invisible hand is understood as having considerable responsibility in shaping economic life and generating economic prosperity. This in turn suggests that Judaism should develop an appreciation of the place of spontaneity in economic life—the subject of our next chapter.

NOTES

1. For a thorough study of competition and market regulations in Jewish sources see Tamari, *With All Your Possessions*, 83–158.

2. Mishna, *Order Nezikin*, trans. Philip Blakman (London: Mishna Press, 1954), 120.

3. *BT*, Baba Metzia, 60a; R. Yosef Karo, *Shulchan Aruch* Choshen Mishpat, 228:18.

4. Mishna, ibid.

5. R. Yosef Karo, *Shulchan Aruch*, Chosen Mishpat, 228:17.

6. Joseph Menirav, *Prakmatia—The Marketing System in the Jewish Community in Palestine During the Mishna and Talmud Era* (Ramat-Gan: Bar Ilan University, 2009), 242–43.

7. *PT*, Aboda Zara 3:3.

8. Menirav, ibid., 220–24.

9. Tosefta, Demay 5:2, Liberman, 85–86; *PT*, Sota, 9:13.

10. *Mishna*, Babba Batra, 2:3, ibid., 173.

11. *BT*, Babba Batra, 21b, trans. Isidore Epstein (London: Soncino Press, 1990).

12. Menirav, ibid., 242–43.

13. *BT*, Baba Batra, ibid.

14. Ibid.

15. Ibid., likewise see R. Yosef Karo, Shulchan Aruch, Choshen Mishpat, 156:5; R. Moshe Feinstein, Igrot Moshe, Choshen Mishpat 2.31.

16. For more details regarding Herem Hayishuv see Simcha Goldin, *Uniqueness and Togetherness, The Enigma of the Survival of the Jews in the Middle Ages* (Tel-Aviv: Hakibbutz Hameuchad, 1997), 162–74.

17. Rabenu Asher in R. Yosef Karo, *Beit Yosef*, Choshen Mishpat, 156.

18. Goldin, ibid.

19. Bernard Dov Weinryb, *The Jews of Poland: A Social and Economic History of the Jewish Community in Poland from 1100 to 1800* (n.p.: The Jewish Society Publication of America, 1972), 74–76. Jacob Katz, *Tradition and Crisis: Jewish Society at the End of the Middle Ages*, trans. Bernard Dov Cooperman (New York: Syracuse University Press, 2000), 44–51, 170–80.

20. *BT*, Baba Batra 21b–22a.

21. *BT*, Baba Batra 22a.

22. *BT*, Baba Kama 8a.

23. See Maimonides, *Mishneh Torah*, Laws of Witnesses, 3.1; 3.4.

24. *BT*, Baba Batra 8b, see also in Tosefta, (ed. Saul Lieberman) Baba Mezia 11:23.

25. *BT*, Baba Batra 91a.

26. Ibid., 89a.

27. Maimonides, *Mishneh Torah*, Laws of Sales, 14:1–4.

28. See A. H. M. Jones, *The Cities of Eastern Roman Provinces* (1937; repr., Oxford, 1971), 215–19.

29. *BT*, Berachoth 3b, Sinsino,

30. *Republic* 372d–373e.

31. *Republic* 399e, 404d

32. Joshua I. Weinstein, "The Market in Plato's *Republic*," *Classical Philology* 104 (2009): 439–58.

33. See M. I. Finley, *The Ancient Economy* (1973; repr., Berkeley and Los Angeles: University of California Press, 1999).

34. *BT*, Nidah, 70b.

35. *BT*, Yoma 38a–b.

36. *BT*, Baba Batra, 91a.

37. *BT*, Taanith, 23a.

38. Sifre, Deuteronomy, 42.

39. As claimed in Michael Novak, *The Catholic Ethic and the Spirit of Capitalism* (New York: Free Press, 1993), 91–103.

6

SPONTANEOUS ORDER

The lack of an economic theory in Jewish scriptures may seem odd until one realizes that neither the Torah nor the Talmud specifies any rules of order for the polity. The Torah does not teach us about any system of organization of the tribes or about how to elect the elders.[1] While there are some Talmudic references about the relationship between kings and the judicial system,[2] and about the rights of citizens of the city to decide their lives on their own,[3] there is nothing about the way they should vote or how should they elect or choose their leadership.

This void demands an explanation. Both the Bible and the Talmud seem to portray the polity as an amorphous entity, whose existence is independent of any regime. According to the Torah, the Jewish people received the Torah as already existing in some fashion, then wandered forty years in the Sinai desert before conquering the Canaanite land—all without any discernible description of its form of political organization.

The Bible provides little explicit clarification of this conceptual quandary. In some way, "Israel" existed before receiving the law at Sinai, just as it also existed before the anointing of Saul. Despite its extensive legal corpus, the Torah tells us very little about Israel's political structures during those and other periods. Why? Surely we ought not to be satisfied with answers that amount to an evasion of this quandary, such as the claim that the ancient Israelites were, unlike the Greeks, somehow politically immature. Irrespective of the historical reality behind these biblical descriptions, there appears to be a conceptual insistence in the Torah and subsequently about what may be tentatively called "the evolutionarily self-ordering" of Israel that requires elucidation. One way to begin exploring this idea is to examine the use of the biblical category *Kahal*.

One description of the people of Israel is *Kahal*, a category with which the Talmud is also concerned. This category was further employed later in the Middle Ages, and was used to describe a Jewish community, although sometimes with a little twist—the *Kehila*. This chapter focuses mainly on the question of the formation of the *Kahal* as a large political body in the Bible and in the Talmud and explores the political and economic implications that can be derived from it. By doing so, light will also be shed on the character of the smaller political body, the *Kehila*.

The description of the creation of the Jewish nation in the Bible is one of a process: beginning with the forefathers, and continuing to its existence as slaves in Egypt, to its redemption, to the receiving of the laws and a covenant with God, wandering in the desert, and finally to its arrival in the Holy Land. It is a description of a slow process—seemingly a development, rather than an organization that simply resulted from one act. If there is one decisive act, it would be the covenant before entering the land of Israel. However, the covenant with God formed the Israelites not as a corporate body but rather as a *holy* nation. It is this sort of covenant that the Bible is concerned with, rather than a covenant between God and the people out of which a regime is organized.

The crux of our problem is thus that the covenant presumes the existence as the people who enter into it. To define that people as a people—as distinct from a holy nation and a kingdom of priests—no organizing principle or order appears to have been necessary. According to the biblical account, it appears that a spontaneous order will suffice. In fact, we can plainly state that the Torah and the Talmud do not bother themselves with questions of the best regime. They do, however, assume the existence of the people. Determining what regime is best was left to the people.

To the question of *what* the political body is, we are given at least one answer but one that should be understood as a precondition for political organization—the corpus of all Jews living in the land of Israel. While it is true that the Talmud discusses the laws of *Kahal*, it does so also as precondition for establishing a judicial system. In that discussion, there is already a corporate assumption for the *Kahal*: the spatially circumscribed corpus of all the Jews who live in the land of Israel, but the Talmud does not discuss how a *Kahal* should organize itself. Thus, it seems that the *Kahal* evolves spontaneously just as the Israelites did in the biblical descriptions in both Genesis and Exodus, and that the rules of this political organization are left to the discretion of its members.

If there is merit to this argument, then the *Kahal* as a spontaneously defined, nonorganized political body must be clarified. To this end, I will borrow theoretical frameworks derived from the economist-philosopher Friedrich Hayek and the philosopher Michael Polanyi.

A JEWISH SPONTANEOUS ORDER?

According to Hayek, there are two forms of social order—a *spontaneous order* and *an organization*. The *spontaneous order* is an unintended consequence of individual human actions that have no ultimate end in mind; as such, it is a self-generating order. By constast, the *organization* is an artificial order inasmuch as it is a social order intentionally constructed through rules and laws. Whereas *organization* is an order whose elements relate to each other through rules and laws, *spontaneous order* is a natural form of organization where the elements are related through their being, spatially or temporally, parts of the same whole. Many social structures are effects of a *spontaneous ordering*. Hayek, for instance, understood Adam Smith's idea of the invisible hand and the market economy as a type of *spontaneous order*.[4] What Hayek left out is an explanation for *why* some spatial and temporal conditions generate order and some do not.

This chapter attempts to answer this question by adding an element of destiny to the concept of spontaneous order. In this framework, spontaneous orders are generated precisely when people *do* have a common purpose or destiny in particular spatial and temporal conditions, even though—and this is crucial—the purpose may be indifferent to any particular form of political organization.

The theoretical idea of spontaneity in politics was developed throughout the nineteenth century. Ideas of spontaneity in the development of the physical element of the polity—the idea that institutional order may rise spontaneously—enhanced appreciation of spontaneity in law as well. Von Savigny claimed that law, like language, develops naturally. His theory drove him to oppose the legislation of new laws on the grounds that this would be artificial and hence illegitimate. While Savigny looked for the roots of modern German law in Roman law, Otto Gierke held that its roots were in fact Germanic. In Gierke's thought, Germanic law is more fitting to modern law, because unlike Roman law, which is individualistic, the Germanic tradition has elements firmly rooted in the tradition of the corporation, and the idea of corporation is deeply connected to the idea of the mystical body; hence, the physical and the spiritual are intertwined.

Somewhat similar to the arguments of Savigny and Gierke, we may speak of a Jewish spontaneous order, or at least of the legitimacy for a spontaneous order within the Jewish textual tradition, and claim we may that the idea is elaborated on in Jewish thought and *Halakhah*. This is not to suggest that a *theory* of spontaneous order exists in the history of Jewish philosophy or that there is any awareness of one. The contrary is the case. Medieval ideas of rationality did not permit much appreciation for spontaneity. For Maimonides, for instance, wisdom equals order and control. My claim is that spontaneity existed as a stowaway, as a hidden reality within Jewish political theory, and it constitutes an assumption not only in the Bible but also one that Talmudic law cannot do without.

It is also worth noting that while the *theory* of spontaneous order is modern, and while there was no conscious idea of spontaneous order expressed in Jewish philosophy through the Talmudic and Medieval periods, the *idea* of the political as an organically emerging, harmonic corpus of tradition is not new. It existed in those medieval streams of political thought in which Christian theologians described the polity as a mystical body and included the state and the church as one unit. Engelbert of Volkersdorf (1250–1311) used the term "Body Moral and Politic,"[5] while Ptolomaeus of Lucca (1227–1327) pursued the thought that the life of the state is based on a harmony analogous to that of a harmony of organic forces.[6] From the perception of the political as one unit, medieval theologians developed an idea of the individual and his relationship with the political body. That spontaneity was an underlying option for Jewish political philosophy, then, may not be as anachronistic as it seems.

Here it is suggested that the *Kahal* should be defined mainly as a *spontaneous order*. Of course, *Kahal* is not meant to organize itself only spontaneously; rather, the *spontaneous order* refers to a condition—a platform upon which the political body arranges itself in an organized fashion.[7] Only after we recognize that the Torah assumes a *spontaneous order* can we ask whether the Torah also requires any sort of specific regime, or alternatively whether the Torah left the specific form of any regime to the discretion of the members of the body politic. My claim is that the latter is correct.

THE FORMATION OF THE JEWISH NATION: A COVENANT OF DESTINY

As historians of the Bible point out, there is no description of either permanent leadership or political organization in early Israelite history. The tribes simply rallied around the Ark of the Covenant.[8] This notion of a common ideal, in this case the covenant with God, is obviously very powerful and is elaborated on in several places in the Bible. The most explicit statement of this sort is a previously cited passage from the Torah that announces the time when the children of Israel became a nation: "Moses and the levitical priests spoke to all Israel, saying: Silence! Hear, O Israel! Today you have become the people of the Lord your God" (Deut. 27:9).

This special foundational moment took place when the covenant with God was established, as the Torah says: "These are the terms of the covenant, which the Lord commanded Moses to conclude with the Israelites in the land of Moab, in addition to the covenant, which He made with them at Horeb" (Deut. 28:69).

The decisive moment at which the Israelites became a people of the Lord is the moment the covenant was accepted. The covenant is the only *order of organization* that the Torah demands, but, as already noted, this order of organization is between the Jewish people and God. It is not an agreement among the people themselves—it presumes their existence as a people prior to it. To define the Jewish people as a people, no organizing principle or order is necessary; evidently, spontaneous order suffices. The covenant is, therefore, a covenant of destiny, as Rabbi J. B. Soloveitchik defines it,[9] designating the peoples' end rather than its beginning.

One should not conclude from the fact of this people's existence prior to the covenant that this people were without destination. On the contrary, the destination was not decided on at the moment of the covenant. Rather, the destination was in the hearts of the people from the very beginning of the Jewish nation, represented biblically in the promise to Abraham. Once again, their destination did not imply, let alone embody, any obvious form of political organization.

The Jewish nation is described as being descended both from the forefathers—Abraham, Isaac, and Jacob—and the Israelites assent to the covenant with Moses. What constituted the people of the Lord was the covenant or covenants with God. That is the reason why belonging to the Jewish nation is not a matter of race. It is a matter of a special relationship between God and the Jewish people and of a covenant with the forefathers, Abraham, Isaac and Jacob. As the Torah states:

> It is not because you are the most numerous of peoples that the Lord set
> His heart on you and chose you—indeed, you are the smallest of peoples;
> but it was because the Lord favored you and kept the oath He made to your
> fathers that the Lord freed you with a mighty hand and rescued you from
> the house of bondage, from the power of Pharaoh king of Egypt.[10]

The source of this relationship is God's love and favor toward the Jewish nation; it is a relationship that one can never escape.

A nation that is formed through covenant, even a covenant of destination, is not solely a derivation of a single act. It is not only the covenant that formed the Israelites as a nation but a slow evolution of one destiny—the worship of God. Thus, one should not view the covenant at Mt. Sinai as the founding constitutional moment of the polity of Israel. The destination of the Israelites had started already with the forefathers as the people of the Lord, and continued with the redemption from Egypt. The story portrayed in Genesis is one of a family in which some continued the dynasty while others left. The members that stayed are the ones that continue to be connected with God and obey his moral obligations.

This covenant did not cease to affect the children of Abraham. Already in Egypt, when Moses demanded that the Israelites will be let go from Egypt, he did not demand a national freedom but the liberty of worship. As God requested from Moses to demand from Pharaoh: "And say to him, 'The Lord, the God of the Hebrews, sent me to you to say, Let my people go that they may worship me in the wilderness'" (Ex. 7:16). The request that God demanded was not only to let the people go but to let them go that they might worship God in the wilderness. It is for this destiny that the Hebrews left Egypt, and it is this destiny that formed them into a holy nation. The covenant was only a crucial moment in a very long process of a destiny that crystallized in time. It may be noticed that Moses never demanded from Pharaoh to let the people go so that the Israelites might live in the land of Israel. It so happened, but it was *not* the destiny specified at that time. Nevertheless, being in the land of Israel was, as we will see, a formative element.

KAHAL, ERETZ ISRAEL, AND THE
INSTITUTIONS OF THE STATE

According to Hayek, a *spontaneous order* must exist before any organizational order can be established. This *spontaneous order* has internal rules and evolves in space. While the rules are difficult to locate, the space must be defined. In Jewish law, the spatial element of *Kahal* is very clear: in order to become *Kahal* the Jewish people must live in Eretz Israel. This spatial precondition is applied in two cases—to both the judicial system and the kingship. Although it seems that the spatial element is independent, I would like to show that this element embodies a destination as well.

Maimonides holds that the obligation to establish a judicial system exists only in the land of Israel.[11] As such, it may be seen as one implication of applying the principle of *Kahal*. The source of this contention is talmudic, as the Talmud says: "[t]hey (the settlers of the land of Israel) are called *Kahal*. Others are not called *Kahal*."[12] The law that contains the definition of *Kahal* does not specify any necessary rules of organization. It does not matter whether the corpus of the people has a formal leader or even whether the people organize themselves formally at all. The only feature of any consequence is that they, as a *Kahal*, settle within the same land.

As David Henshke pointed out, Maimonides' definition of the Jewish nation is strongly connected to Eretz Israel.[13] Maimonides derived his idea from the Talmudic rule that only the Jews living in Eretz Israel are considered *Kahal*. This requirement is raised in the context of a Talmudic discussion on the authority of the Sanhedrin. The Torah states that when the whole Jewish nation sins, there is a national obligation to offer a special sacrifice:

> If it is the whole community of Israel that has erred and the matter escapes the notice of the congregation (*Kahal*), so they do any of the things that by the Lord's commandments ought not to be done, and they realize their guilt—when the sin through which they incurred guilt becomes known, the congregation shall offer a bull of the herd as a sin offering, and bring it before the tent of meeting.[14]

The Talmud elaborates on this, teaching that the error of the whole community of Israel is necessarily an error assisted by the community's teachers. A multitude escapes noticing a law only due to inadequate instruction by the institution in charge of teaching the laws—in this case the Sanhedrin. The collective may, of course, err on its own accord, but because we assume that the masses are not intellectually self-sufficient and that they rely on the teaching of the Sanhedrin, we assume that the errors of the collective are caused by the latter.

According to the Talmud, the Sanhedrin is assumed to be the official judicial body of the *Kahal*, and the Sanhedrin receives its authority from the *Kahal*. That is why the Sanhedrin's rulings are valid only if they are followed by the *Kahal*.[15] It is therefore essential to understand what *Kahal* is, and the Talmud proceeds to define the *Kahal* as the community of the Jewish people who live in Eretz Israel: "Rav Asi says: Judgment depends on the majority of the settlers of the land of Israel ... they (the settlers of the land of Israel) are called Kahal. Others are not called Kahal."[16]

The *Kahal*, for these purposes, is comprised only of Jews who live within the borders of the land of Israel.[17]

The link between *Kahal* and Sanhedrin goes both ways, as Maimonides contends; for not only is the *Kahal* the corpus that confirms the judgment of the Sanhedrin, but it is also the *Kahal* who appoints the Sanhedrin:

> And I hold that if there will be an agreement of all the students and sages to appoint a man in the Yeshiva, meaning, to make from him a head, and on the condition that it will be in the land of Israel, as we said in the introduction, this man will have a yeshiva and will be authorized, and will appoint any one he pleases.[18]

Unlike the common tradition assuming that *Semikha*, the authority to judge and deliver rulings, is from above, from teacher to student, Maimonides asserts that it can be administered from below. A rabbi can be appointed by election of the students and the Sages in the land of Israel. They may decide who the authorized Rabbi will be, and their decision is equal to granting *semikha*. Appointing a rabbi is therefore a democratic act. Maimonides says elsewhere that the reason for the condition that only students and Sages from the land of Israel can appoint a head is that only the Jews who live in the land of Israel count as *Kahal*.[19] This idea of Maimonides' became very famous in the sixteenth century when R. Yaakov Bey Rav appointed himself as a head of the Rabbis, and after being accepted by Tzfat's Rabbis and the majority of the Rabbis in Israel, he appointed other Rabbis as *Semuchim* (R. Yoseph Karo was among them).[20] His action prompted strong opposition by the Jerusalemite Rabbi—R. Levi Ibn Chabib, which is known as the controversy over the *Semicha*.[21]

It is important to note another ramification of the link between *Kahal* and the land of Israel. According to Maimonides, the existence of a Jewish calendar depends on the existence of certified Rabbis. For him, the Jewish calendar does not exist automatically; it is a product of the judgment of the Sanhedrin, which is based either on astronomical observations or on astronomical calculations. However, Maimonides adds that without the existence of Jewish people in the land of Israel, there is no Jewish calendar.[22] As Henske has shown, the awareness of the Jewish calendar in the eyes of the Jewish people in the land of Israel is decisive for the constitution of the Jewish calendar. The reason is, once again, that the only factor that is decisive for becoming the Jewish people as a people is being in the land of Israel. Henshke, therefore, considers this part of Maimonides' argument to be decisive.[23] As he claims, only if one holds (as Maimonides does) that it is only because the Jews who live in Eretz Israel are considered a people and not mere individuals that we can link the existence of the calendar to the Jews living in Eretz Israel.

Thus far, we have seen how both the judicial system of the *Kahal* and its calendar are dependent on a spatial character of the *Kahal*. What needs to be asked is whether or not the *Kahal* has any *political* significance, not just judicial.[24] The question of whether or not there is any idea of spontaneous political order in Halakhah still requires elucidation.

KAHAL AND KINGSHIP

At this point, focusing on the positive obligation to establish political leadership and other obligations that pertain to the Jewish people in the land of Israel may help us to understand better the relationship between *Kahal* and the land. In Talmudic law, no national obligation applies to the Jewish people until it is situated in the land of Israel. The Talmud, for instance, says that three commandments were given to the Israelites when they entered Eretz Israel: to appoint a king, to destroy the Amalekites, and to build the temple.[25] These commandments are also repeated in Maimonides' writings.[26] The commandment to appoint a king is not valid in the Diaspora despite the fact that this may have been possible and that some sort of kingship did exist in exilic history. The Jews in Persia during the Talmud throughout the Geonic period had a leader, the Exilarch who served as the Jewish minister in the Persian court.[27]

It is worth noting that the obligation to appoint a king is valid only when the existence of a nation, a people in its land, can be assumed. We know this from the way the Sages treat the obligation to appoint a king. They argue whether this is a positive obligation or whether it is simply a deterrent.[28] The Rabbis can certainly imagine a nation without a king. Their argument is about whether this obligation is a positive value for the nation or not, and yet it is clear to all that the appointment of a king does not constitute the nation, just as destroying the Amalekites or building the temple do not constitute the nation.[29]

Thus, we see that the two institutions, the judicial system and kingship, are both conditioned with a spatial element, the situation of the nation in Eretz Israel. We may still ask why this spatial element is so important and whether it is only spatial.

THE CASE OF THE KEHILA

The case of the *Kehila*—the Jewish community—is very similar to that of the *Kahal*. Like the *Kahal*, *Kehila* suffers from a lack of organizational order; nonetheless, it is considered holy as well, precisely as *Kehilat Kodesh*.[30] Of course, it is the sanctity of the *Kahal* that inspired the Jews in the Middle Ages to attribute this sanctity to the *Kehila*. Not surprisingly, however, *Kehilat Kodesh*—like *Kahal*—is organized spontaneously. There is no need for a formal method of organization in order to form a *Kehila*. Living in a space (albeit not Eretz Israel) for one month suffices to obligate one with communal responsibilities, such as those to do with religion or welfare.[31] The spatial element, however, is not the core decisive element that creates the *Kehila*. Apparently, there is no *Kehila* without a covenantal element. The assumption is that all the members of the *Kehila* may be united by a religious faith. Without this faith, the *Kehila* will not be a political entity, simply a commercial unit. The name *Kehilat Kodesh* already conveys that there is a religious element that creates the political corpus that we call *Kehila*.

The way that Jews organized themselves historically shows indeed the importance of spontaneous order and contradicts usual categories of regimes. Yet one might expect that we would find a very developed theoretical discussion over the best regime of the *Kehila*. Alas, except for discussions on the authority of the elected representatives and leaders of the *Kehila*, there are very rare discussions on the question of what is the best way for a community to organize itself. The Halakhah definition of *Kehila* suffers from the same absence of a theory of organizational order. It accords much more to a spontaneous order. Some describe the polity as a partnership or association based on the tacit consent of liberated people to accept rules and leadership. Others like to emphasize the authoritative element—kingship or the judicial court—*Beit Din*. Still, neither the notion of a type of social contract nor *Beit Din* seems to explain fully the concept of *Kehila*. In fact, the existence of *Kehila* is prior to the creation of *Beit Din* by any deliberate social contract. In the Talmud, *Kehila* exists without any preorganization, neither of *social contract* nor of *Beit Din*. Its existence is just assumed.[32]

Beit Din and *association* as Halakhah models indeed have their Talmudic roots. What is missing is the model of the Caravan. According to the Talmud, people who join together to cross the desert are bound as an association by a tacit consent:

> The rabbis taught: "A caravan that was attacked by robbers and one of them succeeds in saving some goods from them, this must be divided among the passengers; if, however, he said to them, 'I will try to save for myself,' it is of avail." Let us see how the case was. If each of them could do the same, but he preceded them even if he has said, "I will save for myself," he must not do so. (It is not of avail because all of them have not renounced the hope of regaining it.) And, on the other hand, if it was impossible for them to save their goods, and the one succeeded nevertheless in saving some, why must he divide among the caravan? (They have already renounced their hope of regaining.) Said Rami bar Hama: "It means when they were partners, and in such a case a partner may separate himself against the will of his partner; therefore if he said, *I will do so*, he is separated; but not if he did it silently." R. Ashi, however, says: "The case was that they could save only with great trouble. If he did it silently, he must divide; but if he said, *I will take the trouble on myself*, it is of avail."[33]

This quotation was used since the twelfth century as a source for the power of the community over the individual. The Jewish community in the Middle Ages perceived itself as a caravan, struggling to survive in a unfriendly environment.

The emphasis on the fact that such an association is done tacitly is crucial here. It means that the community as an association is not created in a deliberate fashion but tacitly, or as a spontaneous order.

What is the reason for the absence of an organizational order theory in Halakhah? The importance of a common destiny provides a good answer to the question. However there is also a practical one: We find the definition of the *Kehila* in the answers of rabbis from questions posed by members of the *Kehila* who questioned the legitimacy of their leadership. The questioners never asked for *a priori* instructions about how a Jewish community should organize itself in the future. The questions are always *a posteriori*: that is, after the community is already in existence; only then did they ask for legitimacy. This sort of procedure is not surprising. The place of Jewish law is not to constitute the communal organization but to regulate it.[34] Jewish law does not try to constitute a community anew but to qualify and to regulate the rules of an already existing community. This, in turn, leads to an even stronger claim, from a meta-Halakhah point of view—Halakhah itself is developed spontaneously within an evolving tradition. The lack of an organized constitutional framework resulted in a system that is much more spontaneous, just like the common law system, whereby laws are developed through discussions and decisions of jurists and not by official legislators. No wonder such a spontaneous organizational system of law does not develop an organizational political order. A spontaneous legal system produces a spontaneous political system.

THE MARKET AND ITS DESTINY

The market is not seemingly a place of spiritual aspiration, and the marketplace is not Mount Zion. If spontaneity is generated from space and destiny, what destiny do we find in the market? We might suggest prosperity as destiny; prosperity, with all that enables and reflects, is, however, just a device. Judaism as a religion does not perceive prosperity in this world as a value of its own. When the Torah promises prosperity in the land of Israel, it is not prosperity that is a goal but rather that which can be achieved by this prosperity. Nonetheless, prosperity can become a destiny; if not as an ultimate goal, as a vehicle for a life of real value.

Prosperity is indeed a destiny for whoever is involved in the market, and successful businessmen are only those for whom prosperity is a destiny. The problem with such prosperity is that it is not long lasting, but prosperity as a goal does not have to be an ultimate goal. Even if destiny is a secondary goal as a stepping-stone for achieving an end that is much more valuable, it provides the vector necessary for success. That is why God promises prosperity in the land in Deuteronomy:

> And it will come to pass that if you continually hearken to My command-
> ments that I command you today, to love the Lord your God, and you serve
> him, with all your heart and with all your soul—than I will provide rain for
> your land in its proper time, the early and late rains, that you may gather

in your grain, your wine, and your oil. I will provide grass in your field for
your cattle and you will eat and be satisfied.[35]

As Maimonides explains, this promised prosperity is not a goal for its own sake
but a means for spiritual achievement:

> Once it is known that a reward is given for fulfilling commandments and
> that the goodness which we will receive if we follow the way of God as
> mentioned in the Torah is life in the World to Come, as it is written, "…
> that it may be well with you, and that you may prolong your life," and that
> the revenge which shall be unleashed upon the wicked people who disre-
> garded the righteous mannerisms as mentioned in the Torah is excision,
> as it is written, "… that soul shall utterly be cut off; his iniquity shall be
> upon him"—then what is it that is written in throughout the Torah, that if
> one listens, one will receive such-and-such, and that if one doesn't listen
> such-and-such will happen to one, as well as all earthly matters such as
> plenty, famine, war, peace, monarchy, humility, living in Israel, exile, suc-
> cess, misfortune and other covenantal matters? All these matters were true
> and always will be. Whenever we fulfill the commandments of the Torah
> we will receive all good earthly matters, and whenever we transgress them,
> all the mentioned evils will befall us. Nevertheless, the goodness is not all
> that the reward for fulfilling commandments consists of, and the evils are
> not the entire punishment received by transgressors. This is how all matters
> are decided: The Holy One, Blessed Be He, gave us this Torah, which is a
> support of life, and anybody who does what is written in it and knows that
> everything contained in it is complete and correct, will merit life in the
> World To Come. He will merit [a portion] in proportion to the magnitude
> of his actions and to the extent of his knowledge. The Torah assures us that
> if we fulfill it with joy and pleasure and always act according to it, then
> all things such as illness, war, famine, et cetera, which could prevent us
> from doing so will be removed, and all things such as plenty, peace, rich-
> ness, et cetera, which will aid us in fulfilling the Torah will be influenced
> to come our way so that we will not have to occupy ourselves all day in
> [obtaining] bodily needs, but that we will be free to sit all day, learn and
> gather knowledge and fulfill commandments, in order to merit life in the
> World To Come. In this vein it is written in the Torah after the assurance
> of goodness in this world, "And it shall be accounted virtue in us, if we
> take care to do all these commandments before the Lord our God, as He
> has commanded us." The Torah also tells us that if we willingly neglect the
> Torah to pursue valueless activities, like it is written, "But Jeshurun grew
> fat, and kicked," that the True Judge removes from the transgressors all the
> goodness of this world which they had in their possession but rejected, and
> will bring upon them all the evils which will prevent them from attaining
> life in the World To Come, so that they will be lost in their wickedness.
> It is written, "Because then would you not serve the Lord your God …
> therefore shall you serve your enemies which the Lord shall send against
> you." It would seem that all the blessings and curses are fulfilled in this

manner, namely that if one serves God with joy and follows His ways one will be blessed accordingly and all the curses will be removed far away from one so that one will be [entirely] free to become knowledgeable in Torah and busy oneself in it, in order to merit life in the World To Come. If one does not acquire wisdom and if one has no meritorious deeds, then with what will one merit life in the World To Come?! For it is written, "... and there is no work, nor device, nor knowledge, nor wisdom, in Sheol." If one ignores God and transgresses by means of food, feasting, adultery or similar activities, then one will bring upon oneself all these curses and remove all the blessings, so that one's days will end in panic and fear and one will not have the opportunities or perfect body to perform mitzvot, and one will not merit life in the World To Come, and then one will have lost out on two worlds, for when someone is troubled in this world by illness, plague or hunger he does not busy himself with learning or commandments, with which life in the World To Come is merited.[36]

Prosperity is never an end for itself; it is only a means for a spiritual end. Nonetheless, even as means, prosperity is an end worth striving for. Entering the market with such a goal does promise success.

CONCLUSION

As we have seen, *spontaneous order* exists in Jewish political theory. Political institutions such as government (or kingship) and the judicial system (or the Sanhedrin) depend on the preexistence of a *spontaneous order* that is based on a spatial condition of Jewish peoples settled in the land of Israel, destined to worship the Lord. The organized bond is the existence of a covenant between the Jewish people and God—a covenant insufficient by itself to constitute nationhood. The assumption is that when the Jewish people settle the land of Israel, there is a unique corpus with added spiritual value that deserves God's attention. As the rabbis say, the Divine Presence sets only in the land of Israel.[37]

As mentioned, it is not only contemporary Jewish philosophy that has failed to address the idea of *spontaneous order*. Medieval Jewish philosophy did not appreciate *spontaneous order*, especially when the subject is intellectual power. The intellect is always organized. Thus, Maimonides depicts God's intellect as the intellect of an architect, the great designer and planner of the world. God's plans are detailed and organized. This sort of intellect, referred to as God, is not qualitatively different from man's intellect; for man's intellect is only inferior to that of God because man arrived in the world after its creation.[38] Maimonides is not interested in describing God as a free artist who permits chance in his artistry. He cannot accept a type of creation that evolves organically through trial and error, despite the way that the Torah itself describes creation. A description of God as a spontaneous artist would, to Maimonides's mind, be an odd idea. Like Maimonides, Maharal also describes the intellect as the source of organization.

Torah for Maharal is the mind (*sechel*), and the mind is order. Everything in the mind is in order without exception. A Torah scholar has to be organized and even his clothing must express his organized nature.[39] It would appear that any attempt to seek appreciation of spontaneous order in the writings of Talmudic Sages would amount to an anachronism.

To the Talmudic eye, however, the cognitive power of the politician is described in a manner that seems more spontaneous:

> And Rava the son of Mechasia said in the name of Rav Chama the son of Guria who said in the name of Rav: if all the waters will be ink, and all the canes will be quells, and the sky parchment and all the peoples clerks, they will not be able to write the volume of the mind of the politician.[40]

Here it appears that we have a description of the politician's mind as approaching the greatness of God's mind, as one can neither speculate about it nor imagine its extent. Yet the divine-like description of the politician's mind was not meant only to augment the importance of the politician. It also served to underscore how infinite it is. By being infinite, the Talmud achieves a nonlinear definition, or in other words, spontaneous order.

What can we deduce from this Talmudic appreciation for spontaneous order? Appreciation in itself does not suffice for an automatic acceptance of the free market as the invisible hand of Adam Smith. We can safely assert that Talmudic thought should be in favor of such policy. Appreciation for spontaneity is appreciation for the hand of God that dwells within the public sphere, be it through politics or society more broadly. It is an appreciation that there is something godly in the public sphere and therefore an appreciation for wisdom that is greater than man can speculate. Hence, while we cannot deduce an *a priori* commitment to the free market from the sources analyzed in this chapter, adapting a policy of a more or less completely controlled market or a planned economy surely contradicts the spirit of Talmudic thought.

NOTES

1. About the elders in the Bible see Michael Walzer, "Biblical Politics: Where Were the Elders?" *HPS*, 3 (2008): 225–38.

2. *BT*, Sanhedrin 18a–b.

3. *BT*, Baba Batra 8b.

4. It is important to note that Hayek was not the first to talk about *spontaneous order*. See for instance Michael Polanyi, *Science, Faith, and Society*, (Chicago: University of Chicago Press, 1946), 63–84. I am grateful to Professor Steven Grosby for pointing out Polanyi's contribution to me.

5. Otto Gierke, *Political Theories of the Middle Age*, trans. Frederic William Maitland (1900; repr., Cambridge: Cambridge University Press, 1968), 24. In the *De Ortu, Progressu, et Fine Romani Imperii Liber* (c. 2) In these writings Engelbert of Volkersdorf shows the origin of all *regna et principatus* to have been in a *pactum subjectionis*. There he expresses the importance of civil contract and of delegated sovereignty.

6. Otto Gierke, ibid, 25.

7. Hayek himself is explicit in saying that a "constitution" is in the regime of organization and not in the regime of spontaneous order.

8. John Bright, *A History of Israel* (London: SCM Press, 1959), 143.

9. Rabbi J. B. Soloveitchik, *Fate and Destiny: From Holocaust to the State of Israel* (Hoboken, NJ: KTAV Publishing, 2000), 42.

10. Deuteronomy 7:7–8. For an early covenant see for instance the covenant of "Brit Bein HaBetarim" the covenant of the halves (Gen. 15).

11. Rambam, Sanhedrin, 1:2. On the other hand see also *BT*, Makot 7a; Nachmanides (Deut. 16:18).

12. *BT*, Horayot 3a.

13. David Henshke, "The Legal Source of the Cocept 'Nation': Between Maimonides and Ramban," in *Shenaton Ha-Mishpat Ha-Ivri*, vols. 18–19, ed. Eliav Shochetman and Shmuel Shilo (Jerusalem: Institute for Research in Jewish Law, 1992–1994), 177–97.

14. Leviticus 4:13–15.

15. Note that what came out of this rule is that there is a link between the Sanhedrin and the *Kahal*, and it goes both ways: The authority of the Sanhedrin is dependent on the people that follow them. Every judgment that is made by the Sanhedrin is dependent on the *Kahal*, and receives its authority from this *Kahal*. According to Maimonides, a decree of the Sanhedrin is dependent for its validity on the question of whether or not the Jewish people follow it: "Indeed if the court made a decree and thought that that the majority of the people will be able to follow it, and after their decree the nation had doubts and the decree did not reach the [following of the] majority of the people, the decree is annulled and they [the Sanhedrin] are not permitted to compel it" (Maimonides, *Mishne Torah*, Hilkhot Mamrim 2:6).

16. *BT*, Horayot 3a.

17 The spatial element is not its only defining characteristic. As the Talmud says, not every Jew who lives within the borders of the land of Israel counts as a member of the *Kahal*. A member of the *Kahal* must be an observer of the laws: "[If any person from the] populace unwittingly incurs guilt by doing [any of the things which by the Lord's commandments ought not to be done and he realized his guilt]" (Lev. 4:27), except of a Mumar. *Babylonian Talmud*, Horayot 2a. The laws of offering a sacrifice for atonement are meant for observers of the laws.

18. Rambam's commentary to the Mishna, Sanhedrin 1:3. See more Rambam, Sanhedrin 4:11.

19. Rambam's commentary to the Mishna, Bechorot 4:3; *BT*, Horayot 1:3.

20. R. Yaakov Bey Rav, Shut Mahari Bey Rav, 63.

21. R. Levi Ibn Chabib, *Shut Maharalbach*, S' 147, Kuntres HaSmicha 1, (Jerusalem: Reem Fund, 2008), 483–578. On the dispute over the Smicha see: Eliav Shochetman, "Renewal of the Semicha According to Maimonides," in *Shenaton Ha-Mishpat Ha-Ivri*, vols. 14–15, ed. Mordechai A. Rabelo and Shmuel Shilo (Jerusalem: Institute for Research in Jewish Law, 1988–1989), 217–43; Chaim Zalman Dimitrovski, "Shtei Teudot Chadashot al vicuach hasmicha bitzfat," in *Sfunot*, vol. 10 (Jerusalem: Yad Ben-Zvi, 1966), 192–93; Meir Bnayahu, "Chidusha Shel Hasmicha Bitzfat," in *Sefer HaYovel Lyitzhak Ber*, ed. Shmuel Etinger, Haim Bienart, and Menahem Stern (Jerusalem: Zalman Shazar Center, 1961), 248–69.

22. Maimonides, *The Book of Mitzvot, Positive Commandment*, 153.

23. Henshke, ibid.

24. Maimonides calls the king's heart: "the heart of all Khal Israel" (Kings 3:6). This sort of locution may prove that the king as a political entity is connected to the political idea of Kahal; however, one may very well say that Maimonides refers to the religious side of the nation that the king expresses, not the political.

25. *BT*, Sanhedrin 20b.

26. Maimonides, *Mishneh Torah*, Kings and Wars, 1:1.

27. *BT*, Horayot 11a–b. On the post of the exalarch see Isaiah M. Gafni, *The Jews of Babylonia in the Talmudic Era* (Jerusalem: Zalman Shazar Center, 1990), 92–104.

28. *BT*, Sanhedrin 20b.

29. Nissim b. Reuben, *Derashot* (Sermons), ed. Leon A. Feldman (Jerusalem, 1973), Derasha 11. Rabbi Nissim Gerondi (Barcelona, 1320–1380) distinguished between the law of the Torah and the law of the king. The law of the Torah is the corpus of political laws that exist in the Torah. The law of the king is the civil law that is legislated in every political entity. The purpose of the laws of the Torah is not to create a just state. For this purpose civil law, the law of the king, suffices. The laws of the Torah, on the other hand, are intended mainly for religious purposes. According to my description, the laws of the Torah apply to the religious corpus of people, the corpus that evolves

spontaneously. The laws of the king are relevant only to an organized order that already assumes the existence of the people. The Torah does not relate to this latter type of organizational order. Organizational, political order is completely voluntary. The Torah relates to *spontaneous order* only, but these two sets of laws are not separate. I would claim that without Jewish Law, civil law has no basis. The justification for civil law is as religious as the religious law itself, since only a set of principles that is founded on the basis of religious law can provide moral basis for civil law. Once there exists a religious law, there is no room for natural law. The distinction between civil law and religious law is therefore artificial.

30. On Kehilat Kodesh see Jeffery R. Woolf, "'Qehillah Qedoshah': Sacred Community in Medieval Ashkenazic Law and Culture," in *Holy People: Jewish and Christian Perspectives on Religious Communal Indentity*, ed. Marcel Poorthis and Joshua Schwartz (Boston: Brill, 2006), 217–35.

31. Tosefta, Bava Metzia 11:23; *TB*, Bava Batra 8a; Rambam, Matnot Aniyim 9:12; Shulchan Aruch, Yore Dea 256:5.

32. See Yitzhak Fritz Baer, "The origins of Jewish communal organization in the Middle Ages" *Binah* 1 (1989), 59–82; Shalom Albeck, "The origins of Jewish communal organization in Spain until the Ramah," *Zion* 25 (1960), 87–93; Samuel Morel, "The Constitutional Limits of Communal Government in Rabbinic Law," *Jewish Social Studies* 33 (1971), 87–119; Menachem Elon, "Authority and Power in the Jewish Community: A Chapter in Jewish Public Law" *Shenaton Ha-Mishpat Ah-Ivri*, vols. 3–4 (1976-1977), 7–34; Abraham Grossman, "The Realationship of the Early Sages of Ashkenaz to the Community Sovereignty," *Shenaton Ha-Mishpat Ah-Ivri*, vol 2 (1975), 175–99; Haym Soloveitchik, *The Use of Responsa as Historical Source* (Jerusalem, 1990); Gerald Jacob Blidstein, "Individual and Community in the Middle Ages: "'halakhic' theory," *Kinship and Consent*, ed. Daniel J. Elazar (Jerusalem, 1981), 215–56.

33. *BT*, Baba Kama 116b.

34. This distinction is developed in J. R. Searle, *Speech Acts* (Cambridge: University Press, 1969), 33–42; and John Rawls, *A Theory of Justice* (Cambridge: Belknap Press of Harvard University Press, Mess. 1971), 56, n. 2.

35. Deuteronomy 11:13–15.

36. Maimonides, *Mishneh Torah*, Laws of Repentance, 9:1.

37. Mechilta, Bo, 1; Ramban, Num. 21:21.

38. Maimonides, *The Guide for the Perplexed* III, 17.

39. Rabbi Yehuda Lowe B'r Bezalel (Maharal from Prague), Netivot Olam, Netiv Hatora, 13; Derech Chaim, 5.

40. *BT*, Shabbat 11a.

CONCLUSION

It is now time to summarize Judaism's attitude to the free market, based on the theological, philosophical, and legal analyses undertaken in previous chapters. As we have seen, it is very difficult to extract a clear economic theory from Jewish sources. We find justification of market regulation on the one hand, a strong idea of property rights, on the other, and some overarching notion of market spontaneity. Can any meaningful conclusion be reached from these conflicting principles?

After considering the various arguments, it is tempting to maintain that Jewish tradition has never been concerned with economic theory or even that it is against the free market. But as argued, to judge Jewish sources correctly, one must avoid the error of anachronism by reading the sources in their historical context. Most importantly, one needs to pay close attention to the underlying principles of Jewish law rather than this or that specific law.

We may safely conclude that Jewish law lacks a blueprint for building a successful market. Then again, it has never attempted to create one. As observed, the only formula that the Talmud offers is theological: If one wants to be rich, one should "engage much in business and deal honestly."[1] At the same time, even the most rudimentary engagement in the business world will fail unless one "pray[s] for mercy from Him to whom all riches belong."[2]

Jewish law is clearly not against all rules. The reluctance to specify economic practice was motivated by theological concerns. Jewish tradition rejects neither spontaneous nor political order. As early as the wanderings in Sinai, the form of the political regime adopted by the Jewish people came from foreign sources. Moses' father-in-law, Jethro the Midian priest, suggested a method for building an efficient judicial system. Kingship was an import from the neighboring states. The Torah saw no harm in importing political formulas from foreign sources, an attitude reflected in the later saying of the Sages: "'Let G-d enlarge [yaft] Japheth': implying, let the chief beauty [yafyuth] of Japheth be in the tents of Shem."[3] The Torah does not aspire to create original formulas for securing the material improvement of life, or the efficiency of the political order. Nowhere does it propound the secret for achieving peace in the case of the polity, or prosperity in the case of the market.

So what then *does* the Torah offer? To answer, let us return to Friedrich Hayek. Hayek claimed that no economic formula suffices to create a healthy economy. The economy relies on the laws; but no law will succeed unless it rests on a sound base of principles. Here we find the Torah's contribution to solving many of our problems.

The Jewish tradition's concern is mainly religious and ethical. In general, it emphasizes legal principles, religious principles, and principles that give guidance on how to live a good and ethical life. Of course what is most important is the way the principles relate to one another and the hierarchy formed between them. Charity is important; but it is qualified by the principle of property rights and is not allowed to redefine justice. It would also seem that the idea of distributive justice conflicts with the Jewish principle of private property.

As I have argued, charity is not the only way to help the needy. Generosity is much more helpful and therefore more valuable. Generosity is performed when the needy get help in such a way that their honor is preserved: that is, through investment. Granting loans to people for the purpose of helping them to restore their status or to help them gain wealth is of much greater moment than giving charity. Charity and generosity help the market because each enhances the sense of growth and prosperity. Generosity is, however, more valuable because it enables people to create their own wealth.

Things become more complicated when we approach the subject of market control. The very principle that protects individuals from competition and gives them the right to demand controls also generates the removal of controls. Those individuals concerned for their private property may demand competition in their pursuit of prosperity. In this case, what wins the day is what is most beneficial in securing more private property for more individuals.

Finally, whether or not we believe in free markets, Jewish tradition has an appreciation for unintended order that is an important element toward accepting a market economy. Human understanding and human achievement are in every age qualified by the principles of Jewish law.

Does all this add up to unambiguous Jewish support for a free market? This is unclear. My uncertainty is not because there is anything intrinsically wrong with the freedom of the market but rather because there is a problem with viewing a free market as a formula that purposively *guarantees* prosperity. In the final analysis, *nothing* can guarantee success. In the end, what Jews must do is "engage much in business and deal honestly," as well as to "pray for mercy from Him to whom all riches belong."[4]

NOTES

1. *BT*, Nidah 70b.

2. Ibid.

3. *BT*, Megila 9b.

4. *BT*, Nidah 70b.

About the Author

Joseph Isaac Lifshitz is a Senior Fellow in the Shalem Center in the Department of Philosophy, Political Theory, and Religion. He studied at the Hebron Yeshiva and received his PhD in Jewish Thought from Tel Aviv University. His areas of research include Jewish philosophy, Talmud, Jewish law, Jewish history, and Political Theory. In his study of Jewish Philosophy and history, his main focus is on the philosophy and history of Ashkenaz in the high Middle Ages. He is also a Rabbi of a community in Jerusalem.